CAPE ODD

Strange & unusual stories about Cape Cod

Front Cover

The mysterious twin stone arches on Tupper Road in Sandwich seem almost like some star gate opening to the past. Not some abandoned remnant of a lost culture, the structures were built in the 1920's by an Italian immigrant named Pedro Auriliano. They marked the entrance to his property and may have been constructed to showcase his masonry skills.

Today they stand partially overgrown with wisteria, like some local version of Stonehenge, another odd and unusual piece of Cape Cod history.

CAPE ODD

Strange & unusual stories about Cape Cod

By
Jim Coogan & Jack Sheedy

HARVEST HOME BOOKS
East Dennis, Massachusetts

Cape Odd
First Printing – October 2010

Published by
Harvest Home Books, P.O. Box 1181
East Dennis, Massachusetts 02641

Copyright 2010 by Jim Coogan & Jack Sheedy

No part of this book may be reprinted or reproduced
in any form without written permission from the authors,
except for brief passages quoted as part of a review in a
newspaper or magazine. For information contact
Harvest Home Books at the address above.

ISBN 978-0-9672596-8-0

Cover design and text layout by Kristen vonHentschel

Printed in the United States of America

Additional copies of Cape Odd,
and the authors' previous Cape Cod books,
may be obtained by contacting Harvest Home Books.

Cape Cod Harvest
(Coogan & Sheedy)

Sail Away Ladies
Clarence the Cranberry Who Couldn't Bounce
Priscilla the Amazing Pinkywink
(Coogan)

Dennis Journal
(Sheedy)

Visit us at www.harvesthomebooks.com

Contents

Introduction

Part of the enjoyment of researching a topic is when it takes you down an unexpected path to something unusual and different. With Cape Cod, it's like Forrest Gump's box of chocolates. You never know what you are going to get.

Cape Odd is a collection of what some might call loose ends – snippets of history that may seem insignificant and even trivial. But in the aggregate, these bits and pieces blend into the fabric of the Cape's history and add flavor to the record of the area's past. And we did not want them to be forgotten.

In two decades of culling archives for material in our other books, we've naturally come across information that either didn't fit our theme or that couldn't stand alone as full stories. We saved the things that we found – humorous, unusual, poignant, and strange – with the intent of one day putting them all together in a book. And this is what you now have in your hands.

Cape Odd is broken into chapters that reflect an avenue of associated items. From an opening snapshot summary of the varied activities in a day in the life of 19th century Cape Cod, to topics like crime, religion, sports, and the effects of dealing with Mother Nature's wrath, the book finishes with heartfelt observations about life by Cape Codders both living and dead. In between, *Cape Odd* highlights some of the firsts, the lasts, and the unusual and unique things that make Cape Cod so special. The quirks, foibles, and eccentricities of flag pole sitters, misbehaving Pilgrims, miscalculating pot smugglers, fish eating cows, and a Civil War soldier who persuaded his town to buy him a set of false teeth so he could enlist fill the pages of the book.

We've listed the sources of our information so that you can delve further into an area that might be of particular interest. It's been a lot of fun for us in assembling and releasing this collection of otherwise forgotten obscurities. We hope you will enjoy our efforts.

Jim Coogan
September, 2010
Sandwich, Massachusetts

Foreword

Back in 1880, a waterspout formed over Buzzards Bay and eventually struck land at Barlows Landing in Pocasset where it did a fair amount of damage with its violent windstorm and accompanying hailstones. It was said to have ripped up sod, toppled stonewalls, and destroyed a small boat. It was also said to have levitated a cow belonging to a local sea captain, returning the bovine safely to terra firma. How odd…

This book began for me one sunny November morning over coffee and muffins at a local eatery. On that fall morning, Jim Coogan, my co-author on three previous books, presented an idea for a new book to feature short vignettes concerning somewhat odd and forgotten moments from Cape Cod history. These would be strange and unusual items not typically found within the pages of local history books. Instead, these would be a smattering of stories to form a new and somewhat whimsical layer of Cape Cod history to be placed upon the firm bedrock of the more established local history.

And so began a fall, winter, spring, and summer of research, writing, editing, and further editing toward producing the volume you now hold in your hands – our fourth collaborative effort over these past dozen years. At first the task seemed a bit daunting – to produce a Cape Cod book positioned off center of the more traditional themes – but soon bits and pieces of stories began to form, and the stories began to assemble into themes, and the themes began to arrange themselves into chapters. Before long, it all came together.

Cape Cod history is indeed multilayered, and is, indeed, ongoing. Even today, local history is being made. Local characters continue to breathe life into this peninsula. One has to chuckle at the thought of some writer, fifty or one hundred years from now, researching our feats of today, our successes and failures, and putting them down on paper for others to read. The good, the bad, and the odd.

Jack Sheedy
September, 2010
Dennis, Massachusetts

CHAPTER 1
A Day in the Life

It is difficult to see life through the eyes of people who lived in an earlier time. Our world is not their world. And yet, if we look at events as they were covered in old books and newspapers, we can see that our ancestors had a lot in common with us. They got married, raised families, and bought and sold houses, horses, and ships. They debated the issues of their day, had marital and financial troubles, and experienced the joys of life and the sadness of death. As we look at some of these "slices of life" from another era, we might see our own world reflected in a sepia mirror.

■ ■ ■

In the days before television news coverage, and a century and a half before online news, the local newspaper was the trusted sage of the populace. All the information of relevance to the average Cape Codder was printed in black and white for all to see.

Nowadays, a perusal of newspapers from centuries ago is like a window open upon a long departed time, providing the reader/researcher with a flavor of what life must have been like for those who lived on the Cape in those days. For example, the following items appeared in the Thursday Evening, November 4, 1841 edition of the *Yarmouth Register* newspaper. But first, we may need a little help with terms and abbreviations that might not be familiar to the modern reader:

Glossary of Abbreviations & Terms
    ar – arrived; arrival of a ship
    bbls. – barrels
    brig – a two-masted, square-rigged ship

J. G. RYDER,

Jeweler AND Optician.

Fine Repairing

In all its branches.

MAIN STREET, OPP. BANK.

HARWICH - - MASS.

BEN L. BARDWELL,

DEALER IN

Confectionery · Fruit · Tobacco

AND **Cigars.**

Philadelphia

Ice Cream,

AND

Wellfleet Oysters furnished in any quantity in their season.

Billiard and Pool Room up stairs.

Main Street, opp. Exchange Building, Harwich Centre, Mass.

COURTESY WILLIAM BREWSTER NICKERSON ROOM, CAPE COD COMMUNITY COLLEGE

Harwich, Dennis and Chatham Directory, 1901, page 18.

burthen – ship cargo capacity
in co with – in company with
inst. – instant; occurring during the present month
lat – latitude; distance from the equator in degrees
lon – longitude; distance from prime meridian in degrees
O. – ocean
schr or sch – schooner; two-masted, fore and aft rigged ship
sp oil – sperm whale oil
spoke – two vessels meeting at sea to exchange information
ult. – ultimo; occurring during the previous month
&c. – etcetera

■ ■ ■

A terrific storm on October 3, 1841 ravaged local seafaring interests, drowning 57 fishermen from the town of Truro alone. In the newspaper were listed these items under the category "Marine List:"

"The following account of the recovery of the bodies of three persons lost in the late gale, is furnished by William Hamilton, Coroner at Chatham:

"Oct. 14 – The body of a man was found in the surf at Chatham, by Capt. Richard Gould and others. – The clothing was mostly washed from the body, and no marks could be discovered by which the deceased could be identified. He was supposed to be a man from 30 to 40 years of age."

"Oct. 22 – The body of a man was found by Obed Harding. Had on a long Tom & Jerry coat of dark claret colored cloth, lined with flannel of domestic manufacture – blue and white mixed socks, having W. marked in the tops with white woolen yarn – a striped Drilling shirt, and a red flannel do – a green bocking and black velvet collared jacket. Supposed to be a young man, say 20 or 25 years old."

"Oct. 25 – The body of a man was found by James Bearse, at Monomoy. Had on full suit of oil clothes, with boots, green jacket, two shirts, trowsers, drawers, &c. No marks on the cloth. The letters FRE. were cut on a leather belt buckled round his body. Supposed his age to be 30 or more."

And also this, of a derelict adrift, another victim of the storm:

"The wreck of the schr *Friends' Delight*, of Dennis, full of water, rigging gone from the mast heads, and foremast out of step, was passed recently in lat 40 50, lon 68 47, by brig *J.H. Cheeny*, at Tarpaulin Cove."

■ ■ ■

Yet, amidst all the sad news, a glimmer of hope for one Harwich vessel commanded by a Captain Eldred:

"Schr *Nancy,* Eldred, lost her foremast in the late Westerly gale, and put into Mattapoisett, 28th ult. for a new one."

■ ■ ■

And apparently, not all damage and loss from the storm was restricted to the ocean waves as evidenced by this notice:

"Horse Strayed Away! Some of the fences at Great Island were blown down by the late gale, and an Old Light Red Horse strayed away. Said Horse had a white spot in his forehead, and one white foot. Any person who will notify the Subscriber where said Horse can be found, shall be suitably rewarded. Judah Baker. South Dennis, Oct 28, 1841."

■ ■ ■

The shipping news was of great interest to locals, as many had family and friends at sea. Others had financial interest in the successful completion of a particular voyage perhaps as ship owners or stockholders. Many of these ships were fishing vessels and whalers, while others carried cargoes along the Atlantic coast and across the ocean to Europe in an age predating the clipper ships to arrive on the scene beginning in the 1850's.

For instance, the news from Provincetown, beginning with the brig, *Franklin,* under the command of a Captain Soper:

"Nov. 1 – Ar brig *Franklin,* Soper, from South Atlantic Ocean, with 220 bbls sperm oil. Spoke 29th ult. lat 41 40, lon 65 25, brig *Elba,* Purkis, 18 days, from Pictou for Providence."

"Also, ar brig *Fairy,* Genn, from South Atlantic O., with 220 bbls sp oil."

"30th ult. – Ar schr *Belleisle,* Cook, from South Atlantic Ocean, 170 bbls sp oil."

■ ■ ■

And under the category "Whalers" came news of the departure of two vessels:

"Sailed from Falmouth, 23rd, (and from Tarpaulin Cove, 25th, in co with ship *Chris Mitchell*), ship *W. Penn,* Lincoln, Pacific Ocean."

■ ■ ■

Anchor dragging was a profitable business along the backside of the Cape, where vessels wrecked and where anchors and chains could become lost:

"Notice. Picked up in the surf back of Cape Cod, abreast of South

Wellfleet, on the 5th inst. by George Ward and others, a chain and two anchors, which the owner can have by proving property and allowing salvage. South Wellfleet, Oct 11, 1841."

■ ■ ■

Vessels were bought and sold on a regular basis, and were advertised as such, not unlike today's automobiles listed in the classified section of the local newspaper:

"For Sale. The Schr *Two Brothers*, 70 tons burthen, and 10 years old. Said Schr is well found in cables, anchors, sails, rigging, &c. &c., and is warranted free from worms; and has lately been caulked and otherwise repaired and overhauled. Those wanting to purchase such a vessel will do well to call and examine for themselves, as the above vessel is offered to close a concern. Inquire of Josiah Hardy, Jr. Chatham, Oct. 14, 1841."

Or perhaps something a bit smaller:

"For Sale. The well known sch *Wellington*, 66 tons burthen, light draught of water, new topped the last season in the most thorough manner. Said Schr is in every respect well calculated for the mackerel fishery or the lumber business. For terms apply to Hawes & Taylor, of Nath'l S. Simpkins. Yarmouth Port, Oct. 21."

Neither listing mentioned a price.

■ ■ ■

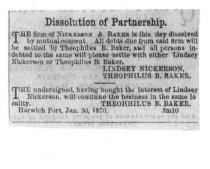

Yarmouth Register, February 25, 1870

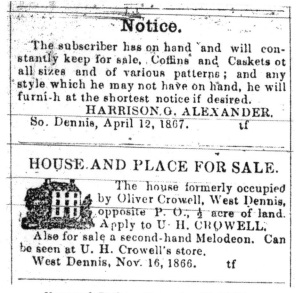

Yarmouth Register, November 22, 1867

Houses were also listed for sale:

"For Sale. The subscriber offers for sale his dwelling house, with about two acres of land, under and adjoining the same, (with a running brook of water at the foot of said land,) situated in the pleasant village of Centreville. Said house is nearly new, and built of good materials, and in the most thorough manner – and is located near the Post Office, Store, Meeting House and School House, and is in all respects a desirable residence for a Mechanic or Sea-faring man – and affords a rare opportunity to procure a first rate location, and on easy terms."

The advert never mentioned the terms, nor did it mention the actual location of the house, although based on its description of being nearby the post office, the store, and the meetinghouse, it most probably resided somewhere along Main Street in Centerville. The listing continued:

"He also offers for sale, either in connexion [sic] with the above premises or separately, his Blacksmith shop and stand, within a few rods of his dwelling, and but a short distance from a Wheelright, and the well known Ship-yard of Mr. Kelley, where vessels are almost constantly building, which with Ship work makes this connexion [sic] with other custom, one of the best Stands for a Blacksmith in the town, there being no Smith of the kind within three miles. Any person desirous to purchase will do well to apply soon, as such an opening rarely occurs. Leander Gage, Centreville, Sept 2, 1841."

Or, if you'd rather a place on the lower Cape:
"House and Land for Sale! The well known residence, in Eastham, of the late Rev. Philander Shaw, consisting of a large Two-Story House, and Barn, with nine acres of good Upland, and one acre of Salt Meadow adjoining. For Terms apply to James H. Knowles, near the premises. Eastham, Oct. 28, 1841."

■ ■ ■

The personal trials and tribulations of Cape residents were spelled out in ink upon the pages of the local newspaper, as displayed in these items on the subjects of love ... and love lost:
Under the category of marriage:
"In Sandwich, last evening, Mr. James Fisher, of Harpers Ferry, Va. to Miss Ellen G. Newcomb, of S(andwich), both deaf and dumb."
And, perhaps, under the category of a spouse gone missing:
"Whereas my wife Keziah Wixon left my bed and board on the morning of the 19th inst, without sufficient cause, and has conveyed herself to parts unknown, I take this method of cautioning all persons against harboring or trusting her on my account, as I shall pay no debts of her contracting after this date. She had on, when she left, a black Circassian cloak, a plain light-colored silk bonnet, and dark calico gown, having previously taken measures to convey away all her wearing apparel. Since that time, although the strictest search and inquiry has been made, nothing has been heard from her. She is a short, thick set woman, has black eyes, black hair tinged with grey, and is dark complexioned. Any person who will inform me of her whereabouts shall be rewarded. Freeman Wixon. South Dennis, Nov 1, 1841."

■ ■ ■

Notice.

RAN away from the subscriber on the morning of Feb. 28th, a bound apprentice, named Oliver Emery, and I hereby forbid all persons harboring or trusting him on my account, as I will pay no debts of his contracting after this date. The above apprentice had lost his first finger on the right hand, to the second joint, is short of stature, light complexion, with large protruding front teeth. I hereby offer one cent reward to any person delivering the above named Oliver Emery to the subscriber.
SAMUEL H. YOUNG.
Chatham Port, Feb. 28, 1870   14

Yarmouth Register, **March 11, 1870**

While, on the subject of finance:

"Assignee's Notice. Notice is hereby given that the third meeting of the creditors of Sanford Herendeen, of Falmouth, in the County of Barnstable, cooper, an Insolvent Debter [sic], will be held at the dwelling house of David Lewis, in said Falmouth, on the tenth day of November next, at two o'clock P.M., when and where creditors can prove their claims, and the Assignee will present his account. George W. Donaldson, Assignee. Falmouth, Oct. 18th, 1841."

"Notice. The Subscribers (in consequence of the ill health of the acting partner) are desirious [sic] of closing their business, and request those indebted to them to make immediate payment, and those having demands to present them for settlement. Their remaining Stock of Goods will be sold Low for Cash. Thomas Akin & Co. So Yarmouth, 10 Mo. 27th, 1841."

■ ■ ■

And, in time of death:

"Melancholy Accident – Mr. Willard Robinson of Falmouth aged 21, while shooting some three weeks since, accidentally discharged his gun and the contents entered under his arm, lodging in the shoulder. Although he received a terrible wound, hopes were entertained of his recovery until Monday the 23rd ult. when symptons [sic] of lockjaw appeared which increased in virulence until Monday the 1st inst, when he expired. All who knew him can bear testimony to his excellence of heart, and heartily sympathize with his afflicted family in their grief at this untimely end."

Finally, this short, sad notice:

"Died ... In Chatham, October 30, Harrison Francis, son of Capt. Franklin and Mrs. Esther Nickerson, aged 11 months and 20 days."

CHAPTER 2
All Along Shore

Cape Cod's connection to the sea has produced its share of unusual stories. Cape Codders have always looked to the ocean for income, adventure, and opportunity. It has been a highway to fame and fortune, but it has also been the scene of disaster and death. From breeches buoy rescues to storm tossed bottles containing messages, the shores of the Cape have always been places of wonder and mystery.

■ ■ ■

Just after the end of the Civil War, Stillman Ellis of Sagamore, a crewman aboard Russell Gibbs' schooner, was loading marble at a Potomac River pier when a group of soldiers came aboard and charged him with the assassination of President Abraham Lincoln. Apparently, Ellis had a close resemblance to John Wilkes Booth. As the story goes, the soldiers examined Ellis' hands and after seeing their roughness, they released the surprised Cape sailor because, as they admitted, no actor would have had rough hands like that. *The Sandwich Independent*, February 9 & 16, 1927.

■ ■ ■

Another Cape Cod mariner who had a brief brush with fame in Virginia was Moses Nye. Mr. Nye was born in Sandwich in 1774. He later married Chloe Gifford of Falmouth and made a number of coasting voyages with his new in-laws. On one trip in 1798 while his ship was passing Mount Vernon on the Potomac River, the crew decided to anchor there to observe the Sabbath. Mr. Nye and two other sailors took a small boat and went ashore. While they were taking their ease under a tree, the owner of the property, ex-President

George Washington, came over to them and asked where they were from. "Falmouth, Massachusetts," the men replied. "I had many a good and brave soldier from your section," the former president told them. And with that, Washington invited the three Cape sailors up to his mansion for dinner. *Yarmouth Register*, May 10, 1940. Mr. Nye's death notice was re-printed in the *Barnstable Patriot*, November 23, 1869.

■ ■ ■

The first steamboat to provide regular service between Hyannis and Nantucket was the 171-ton *Nebraska* (formerly the *Telegraph*). Specially equipped to handle the ice in Nantucket Sound, the *Nebraska* first began service to Hyannis in 1854. *Lifeline to the Islands: Sketches and Memories of Steamers Past and Present on the Woods Hole – Martha's Vineyard – Nantucket Run*, by the Steamship Authority, page 6.

■ ■ ■

Captain Lorenzo Dow Baker of Wellfleet transported his first cargo of bananas from Port Antonio, Jamaica in the summer of 1882. His intent was to reach Boston and sell the fruit there. The bananas began to turn yellow far more quickly than he had anticipated and he had to put in at Jersey City, New Jersey. He received $2.25 a bunch and made a profit of $1,152.05 – the most he had ever made on any cargo. The next trip he made it to Boston with the fruit still green. He sold his cargo to Seaverns & Company and cleared almost $3,000. It was the beginning of the successful Boston Fruit Company, which by the beginning of the 20th century gave Captain Baker the title of "Banana King of Cape Cod." *Dow Baker and the Great Banana Fleet*, by Charles Morrow Wilson.

■ ■ ■

After repeated complaints by people in the village of Buzzards Bay, the Lighthouse Service agreed to get rid of the automatic fog bell. The signal was sounding at all hours even when weather conditions were clear. An operator was assigned to sound the bell by remote control – only when it was really foggy. *Cape Cod News* – Sandwich Edition, June 22, 1938, page 1.

■ ■ ■

On Saturday night, June 20, 1938, President Franklin Delano Roosevelt

A Cape Cod Fisherman

From *Harper's Magazine*, June 1875

found himself stuck at the western end of the Cape Cod Canal. On a return to Washington, D.C. after attending a family wedding in Nahant, a heavy fog set in just as the presidential yacht *Potomac* approached Buzzards Bay. It was decided that because visibility was so bad, the *Potomac* should tie up next to the state pier building for the night. The president never left the yacht during the night and the trip was resumed the next morning at 10:00. *Cape Cod News* – Sandwich Edition, June 22, 1938, page 1.

■ ■ ■

On a spring day in 1941, Antone Merrill, Jr. of Provincetown was walking along the back shore near Highland Light when he spotted a bottle with a note in it. When he pulled out the message, it read: "I wish the party that finds this bottle will have good fishing. I am an American of Irish descent age 40 past. Single and willing to marry. I weight [sic] 140 pounds. I am five feet five inches tall. This bottle was dropped overboard from a fishing boat. Address William Welsh in care of the American consul, Montevideo, Uruguay." *Cape Cod Standard Times*, May 7, 1941.

■ ■ ■

The last use of a breeches buoy in an active sea rescue on Cape Cod happened in January of 1962 when the Provincetown dragger *Margaret Rose* got caught off the back shore in high winds. During that rescue, Coast Guardsman Daniel Davidson from the Chatham station went into the water to rescue a man who was about to drown, having fallen off the stranded vessel. For his heroic action, Davidson received a medal from the Massachusetts Humane Society. From an interview with Daniel Davidson at the Cape Cod Maritime Symposium, May, 2009.

■ ■ ■

A column entitled "A Sailor's advice on courtship," directed toward young women and their path toward maintaining a successful marriage, was printed in *Bostonian* magazine and then re-printed in the December 11, 1839 edition of the *Barnstable Patriot* newspaper:

"My little fair one, as soon as you have entered on board, stand prepared for all kinds of weather, and in every shifting part o the scene, guide your vessel by the rudder of reason. Carefully avoid the rocks of imprudence; run no risk by a prohibited commerce; make no signals nor hang out false colors, but mind to a hair when to traverse or tack, to advance and to retreat, and skillfully steer from the straits of contention. Preserve yourself steady though sirens attempt to seduce you, and by a well-ballasted head secure your heart against the top-gallant delights of the age, which never fail to engage the fresh water fry; and always remember to keep your rebellious passions under the hatches that they may not make a too frightful explosion, and give such a shock to the pillars of wedlock as would discourage your lover and cause him, with full spread of sails, to stand away from the gulf of ruin and destruction."

CHAPTER 3
Fish Stories

Do you ever wonder what lurks in the depths beyond the outer bar? Cast a line and it's anyone's guess what will be on the end when hauled in. Mermaids, sharks, and even sea serpents fill the pages of Cape Cod history. Far from just a few isolated reports, the sightings of strange creatures of the deep are common enough to give a ring of truth to claims that mysterious beings are indeed out there.

■ ■ ■

In an 1875 appraisal of the life of a nineteenth century Cape Cod fisherman, *Harper's Magazine* said, "On this frugal Cape Cod, a fisherman is not unhappy nor unfortunate if he makes five hundred dollars by his year's work. His wife will lay by some of it, and he will subscribe liberally to church and foreign missions, and think himself a comfortable man. He owns his house and little garden patch; he is not afraid of the tax-gatherer; he and his wife know how to make money go far, and they are not at all conscious that they are pinched by poverty." *Harper's Magazine*, June 1875. Article by Charles Nordhoff, Pages 52-66.

■ ■ ■

A Provincetown fisherman named Ellis got a surprise when he examined his catch. Among the fish in his net was a good-sized flounder with his name carved in inch-long capitals on its belly. The inscription appeared to have been carved quite some time before the fish was caught and it had healed up nicely. Witnesses observed that Ellis's name "was as plainly legible as if printed with the blackest printers ink." *Bourne Pioneer*, September 22, 1896.

■ ■ ■

Dogfish "horns" were once used as early phonograph needles.

■ ■ ■

In the summer of 1916, a 15-foot, one-ton, white whale (probably a beluga) became entangled in Gilbert Ellis's East Brewster fish weir. It took the help of two other men, George Le Fort and George Lee, to help Ellis subdue it. The local paper reported, "The strange visitor to our shore caused great excitement in the neighborhood." *Yarmouth Register*, July 1, 1916.

■ ■ ■

Flying Fish: In the "Barnstable Municipal Airport Notes" column during the summer of 1962 were these two items concerning fish: "Aircraft engaged in fish-spotting are congregating here as the season begins. One outfit, Smith Meal Corporation, has a fleet of three small aircraft that start searching for trash fish down in the Gulf and proceed northward until they reach the coast of Maine ... Speaking of fish, a lady in Nantucket is waiting for several 'flying fish' to fly over from the Cape mainland. No joke – They'll be in a tank aboard a Cape & Islands craft." *Barnstable Patriot*, July 5, 1962.

■ ■ ■

In *Mourt's Relation*, a compilation of extracts largely attributed to William Bradford and Edward Winslow, there is a story that the Pilgrims developed a severe case of gastroenteritis after they ate shellfish while the *Mayflower* was anchored in Provincetown Harbor. In the account it was said that they ate "great mussels, very fat and full of sea pearl. They made all sick that did eat, as well as sailors as passengers; they caused to cast and sour. But they were soon well again."

■ ■ ■

Beached whales have been a part of Cape Cod history for as long as humans have lived on this peninsula. In fact, the Pilgrims witnessed beached grampus, or blackfish, in the vicinity of what is now Wellfleet during their first days exploring this New World. As William Bradford wrote in his journal: "They came also to ye place wher they saw the Indans ye night before, & found they had been cuting up a great fish like a grampus, being some 2. inches thike of fate like a hogg..." So, it comes as no surprise, that while scanning a page from an old newspaper, we came across a short mention of a large

GROUP OF CAPE MACKEREL.

From *Harper's Magazine*, June 1875

whale washed up along a Lower Cape beach: "Auto parties during the past few days have been making pilgrimage to Nauset Beach to see a whale which has washed up on the beach. According to the spectacles worn by the visitors the 'big fish' varies in length from 65 to 85 feet and in some instances reaches a height of 70 feet." That certainly was a big "fish" ... or more correctly, mammal. *Hyannis Patriot*, February 5, 1923. Also: *Of Plimoth Plantation*, by William Bradford.

■ ■ ■

The nineteenth century was a time for many sightings of sea serpents around Cape Cod. One of those sightings was made by none other than Senator Daniel Webster. Apparently he was out fishing in the bay and late in the day he and his partner were headed home to Duxbury where the Senator was staying. Webster was known as a tippler and on this hot day it is probable that the two men had had a few. When they made it to shore Webster had second thoughts about going public about his having encountered a serpent. To his companion he said, "For God's sake, never say a word about this to anyone for if it should be known, I should never hear the last of it, but wherever I went I should have to tell the story to everyone I met." Webster's decision to keep quiet about what he may or may not have seen was probably a good idea and undoubtedly saved him from ridicule. His biographer, Claude Fuess admitted that "Under certain conditions, well known to his contemporaries, Dan'l Webster was likely to see several types of reptilia, and I suspect that this occasion may have been one of them." Cited in *Sea Serpents of Coastal New England*, by L.D. Geller, page 13.

■ ■ ■

In the winter of 1939, Coast Guardsmen stationed at the Wood End station in Provincetown reported that they had found the skeleton of a sea serpent cast up on the nearby beach. There was a lot of skepticism about the report. One newspaper noted that "anything can happen at Wood End – and usually does." But the Guardsmen produced a set of bones with 71 vertebrae flanking a long 8-inch diameter spine. No one had any idea what it was and it was shipped to Harvard University for dismemberment and analysis. Eventually professor William C. Schroeder of Woods Hole identified the creature as a basking shark. *Yarmouth Register*, January 27, 1939. Also: *Falmouth Enterprise*, February 3, 1939.

■ ■ ■

Like something out of Barnum and Bailey, an advert from the November 19, 1850 issue of the *Barnstable Patriot* announced that for twenty-five cents admission at Barnstable's Exhibition Hall, one could view a variety of creatures, including elephants, ourang-outangs, and even a "Fejee Mermaid," "which was exhibited in most of the principal cities of America … to the wonder and astonishment of thousands of naturalists and other scientific persons, whose previous doubts of the existence of such an astonishing creation were entirely removed."

■ ■ ■

A mention in the August 2, 1909 *Hyannis Patriot* asked, "Have you seen the mermaid at Bearse's market? It is attracting lots of attention among summer visitors." The creature was apparently caught near Bishop and Clerk's Light, in Nantucket Sound, by Captain Howard Allyn.

■ ■ ■

From the town of Brewster came this report of a mermaid sighting: "A supposed mermaid was seen upon the beach in this village last Thursday by a Mrs. Young and several children. The head of this object, or mermaid, resembled exactly that of a child while the rest of the body was of fish form. When first seen the lady became frightened, but the children, less timid, approached it, and wishing to determine whether it was dead or alive, threw some sand into its eyes, whereupon it uttered cries like that of a child and commenced rolling over and over down to the water and darted off into the sea, keeping its head above the surface and resembling in every manner that of a child swimming." *Harwich Independent*, July 10, 1873.

■ ■ ■

A shark attack on a Navy Lieutenant bathing at Craigville beach in the summer of 1929 attracted a fair amount of attention. Robert B. Yortson, "while swimming out beyond the second or outer float … was attacked by a three-foot shark and bitten on the left hand." The man noticed the shark approaching before it attacked, and seizing upon his Navy training, he hit the shark with his fist on the snout. Unfortunately, the shark was too close and chomped down on his left hand before it departed. Two girls who were on a nearby raft saw the attack. Yortson was able to escape from the shark, and fortunately the injury to his left hand was not serious. Incidentally, the newspaper was quick to point out that Yortson was "a considerable distance out from the bathing beach" when he was attacked, and it was "not known that a shark has ever been seen nearer to the beach." *Hyannis Patriot*, July 25, 1929.

■ ■ ■

An earlier shark attack in Cape waters occurred in 1878 when Woods Hole fisherman Charlie Healy caught "a good sized shark" and then hauled the beast onto his boat. While Healy was reaching for a club "for the purpose of despatching *[sic]* the monster," the shark bit his arm. According to a newspaper report, "Charlie felt the bite very sensibly and soon became faint." What happened next is not quite known. Another fisherman arrived on the scene and attended to Healy's wound. "He is now doing well," reported the paper, although there is no further mention of the shark. *Barnstable Patriot*, September 3, 1878.

■ ■ ■

"Look out ye bathers and not venture too far into the surf lest the shovel mouth devours the pleasure seeker," announced the August

19, 1895 issue of the *Hyannis Patriot*. This warning came from a story that Captain Orrin Nickerson of Cotuit reported he had recently caught a large "Shovel Mouthed" shark the size of a man in his net. Captain Nickerson could not have been too alarmed by the presence of sharks, as it was further reported in the same column that he was to participate in sailboat races off Woods Hole.

■ ■ ■

A toothless 17-foot shark was caught in a weir at Provincetown. Described as a "bone shark ... a species not often found in these waters," it was discovered to be completely devoid of teeth, prompting the newspaper to surmise that it "had evidently been to some dentist, not a tooth being in evidence in either jaw." Yet, it was reported that the shark's liver oil was harvested, "in quantity almost enough to fill two barrels." *Hyannis Patriot*, October 19, 1908.

■ ■ ■

In the summer of 1889, a J. E. Reighard from Michigan University visited North Truro to study "the embryology of the dogfish, a branch of the shark family." Apparently his time at the wrist of the Cape proved to be a fruitless embryological search, as it was reported that, "Finding no specimens of sufficient size in the waters, he has gone to Cape Ann." *Barnstable Patriot*, August 6, 1889.

■ ■ ■

A Cape Cod man had a rare run-in with ancient Mastodons and prehistoric Megalodons, an ancestor of the great white shark, which once swam the oceans millions of years ago. In 1874, Paul Shiverick of Dennis held the position of Superintendent for the Pacific Guano Company, which operated a phosphate mining operation on Chisholm Island, off the South Carolina coast. The phosphate deposits were mined by the company to make fertilizer at a plant on Penzance Point in Woods Hole. According to a newspaper account, "In eighteen month's time [Shiverick's crew] has dyked fifty acres, and with two hundred diggers has supplied the Factories at Woods Hole and Charleston with eleven thousand tons." Within the deposits were found the petrified "teeth of the Mastodon, measuring from six inches to a foot in width, and those of the mammoth shark, the length and width of a human hand." Based on that description, shark teeth of that size would have belonged to a predator some 50 feet in length. *Barnstable Patriot*, October 13, 1874.

■ ■ ■

A crewman aboard the four-masted Dennis schooner *Marjorie* met with a horrible death in the mouth of a killer shark. It seems the crewman refused to perform his shipboard duties and was subsequently put in irons as the vessel, with a cargo of coal, plied its way to Colon (formerly Aspinwall) in Panama. "When ready to leave Aspinwall the prisoner was brought on board and some time during the night tried to steal the vessel's boat and make his escape ... he made haste to enter the boat, but instead fell overboard." According to the vessel's master, a Captain Edwards, the crewman was immediately attacked by a shark and was never recovered. *Barnstable Patriot*, June 30, 1891.

Sorting the Catch. *Cape Cod Magazine*, **August, 1915**

CHAPTER 4
Shipwrecks with a Twist

Over the centuries, some three thousand shipwrecks have occurred along the coastline of Cape Cod, mostly along the backside of the peninsula. Each shipwreck forms a chapter in the history of this storied place. With so many wrecks, some were bound to provide an odd twist or a salty tale, as illustrated by the following from the annals of Cape Cod history and lore. These tales of vessels caught in Neptune's grip provide just parts of their story, as the final chapter for each was not written until days, weeks, months, or even years later.

■ ■ ■

Sparrow-Hawk

Six years after the arrival of the Pilgrims, another band of transatlantic voyagers arrived along the outer Cape coastline, this time with disastrous results. The ship was the *Sparrow-Hawk*, a vessel quite a bit smaller than the Pilgrim's *Mayflower*, and carrying about twenty-five passengers and crew – about a quarter of the complement carried by the *Mayflower* in 1620.

Sparrow-Hawk eventually wrecked at Nauset, as documented by Governor William Bradford in his journal, *Of Plimoth Plantation*. Here are excerpts of that shipwreck, the first such recorded shipwreck along the Cape Cod coastline. This first bit talks of some of the reasons why the ship might have come to woe, whether because of some fault of the captain, or the crew, or even the unruliness of the passengers:

"Ther was a ship, with many passengers in her and sundrie goods, bound for Virginia. They had lost them selves at sea, either by ye

31

insufficiencie of ye maister, or his illness; for he was sick and lame of ye scurvie, so that he could but lye in ye cabin dore, & give direction; and it should seeme was badly assisted either wth mate or mariners; or else ye fear and unruliness of ye passengers were such, as they made them stear a course between ye southwest & ye norwest, that they might fall with some land, what soever it was they cared not."

Bradford continued with his journal entry, painting a picture of a vessel that was out of stores and thus ripe for shipwreck: "For they had been 6. weeks at sea, and had no water, nor beere, nor any woode left, but had burnt up all their emptie caske; only one of ye company had a hogshead of wine or 2. which was also almost spente, so as they feared they should be starved at sea, or consumed with diseases, which made them rune this desperate course."

Eventually, the ship became entangled with the bars off the Cape coast, as Bradford described: "…they came right before a small blind harbore, that lyes about ye middle of Manamoyake Bay, to ye southward of Cap-Codd, with a small gale of wind; and about highwater toucht upon a barr of sand that lyes before it, but had no hurte, ye sea being smooth; so that laid out an anchore. But towards the eveing the wind sprunge up at sea, and was so rough, as broake their cable, & beat them over the barr into ye harbor, wher they saved their lives & goods…"

Word arrived at Plymouth of the plight of the vessel at Nauset, so a number of Pilgrims along with Governor Bradford arrived on the scene to provide assistance to the *Sparrow-Hawk* crew with repairs to their ship. After repairs were made, and "being very thankfull for ye curtesies they received," Bradford returned "thus left them…and so went home" to Plymouth.

■

"But after the Gover thus left them … he had not been at home many days, but he had notice from them, that by the violence of a great storme, and ye bad morring of their ship (after she was mended) she was put ashore, and so beaten and shaken as she was now wholy unfitted to goe to sea." This time the ship was a loss. And so, the *Sparrow-Hawk* crew and passengers joined the Pilgrims at Plymouth for the winter, departing the following year for Virginia.

As for the wreck of the *Sparrow-Hawk*, she was discovered along Nauset Beach in the 1860's and was eventually exhumed and displayed around New England. For a century, the wreck was housed at Pilgrim Hall Museum in Plymouth. In recent years, she has been on loan to the Cape Cod Maritime Museum, located on the waterfront in Hyannis.

"The Lifesavers"
Cape Cod Magazine, **December, 1915**

■ ■ ■

H.F. Dimock

The *H.F. Dimock* was clearly a vessel to be avoided, if at all possible. In July, 1892, while off Chatham, she rammed the 285-foot long, three-masted schooner *Alva*, owned by millionaire William K. Vanderbilt. The *Alva* sank, though all on board were saved. Days later, the *Alva* figured in another collision, when the schooner *Everett Webster* collided with the submerged wreck. Deemed a navigational menace, the *Alva* was eventually dynamited.

A report of the dynamiting of the *Alva* made reference to a leviathan that watched the proceedings: "During the operations of exploding yacht *Alva* Wednesday, a whale about 50 feet long, who had been watching the process, was noticed, after the water had subsided, spouting and plunging and lashing the seas with its tail as if in agony. After about 15 minutes of these antics he made a dart toward the bell buoy, which marks the entrance to Pollock Rip slue and in some way became entangled with it. After a struggle he broke the chain which held the buoy to the rock below and passed out of sight to the eastward, with the buoy still attached to him and ringing harder and louder than it had since the last great storm." *Barnstable Patriot*, May 16, 1893. The *Patriot* report also mentioned that, "A lot of fish were found floating on top of the water after the explosion."

■

As for the *Dimock*, her days of causing havoc were not yet over. In March 1909, in foggy conditions at Pollock Rip off the coast of Chatham, in the very same waters, she rammed another vessel – the *Horatio Hall*. As the *Horatio Hall* began to sink, her passengers and crew were transferred to the *Dimock*, which was also in fear of sinking. To save his vessel, Captain John Thompson ran the *Dimock* aground at Nauset Beach. The following are excerpts from a March 15, 1909 *Hyannis Patriot* article:

"A collision between the two iron steamers, *Horatio Hall*, bound from Portland, Me., for New York with passengers and freight, and the *H.F. Dimock*, from New York to Boston with freight, occurred in a thick fog in the Pollock Rip slue on Wednesday morning ... The passengers (of the *Horatio Hall*) one after another scrambled to the deck of the *Dimock*. Then the crew followed – all except Capt. Jewell, First Officer Parker and First Pilot Snow. These three refused to leave their ship while any portion remained above water ... The *Dimock* then backed away for a short distance and stood by for several hours, the passengers and crew gathering about the rail and watching the *Hall* through the fog as she slowly settled ... When it was finally seen that the *Hall* had struck bottom and was in no immediate further danger the *Dimock* started out to land her passengers before she herself could sink ... just after 2 o'clock the *Dimock* grounded in the sand a few miles off Orleans..."

The *Hyannis Patriot* article referenced the *Dimock's* earlier rendezvous with the *Alva* "seventeen years next July" and stated that "the vessel has been a hoodoo however from the start, and has been in trouble time and again." The article ended with, "No effort as yet has been made to relieve Pollock Rip slue of the sunken steamer *Horatio Hall*, a menace to navigation," but reported that "the *Dimock* was floated Sunday afternoon with the assistance of four large tugs and a lighter, and proceeded to Boston..."

It didn't take long, though, for the *Hall* to become torn apart by the seas: "The storm of Thursday did much damage to the steamer *Horatio Hall*, recently stranded in Pollock Rip slue after being in collision with the *H. F. Dimock*. The vessel is breaking up and quantities of the wreckage is coming ashore." *Hyannis Patriot*, March 29, 1909.

The same article made mention of an interview at Portland, Maine with the *Hall's* former master, Captain Albert Bragg, who visited the wreck, and who "was in command of the *Horatio Hall* in the terrible November storm of 1898, when the *Portland* went down, and in paying tribute to her said her great seaworthiness was well proven that night, when she outrode seas and gales that sent other vessels to port or to the bottom." The article went on to say that Captain Bragg was "actually weeping over the loss of the vessel" and that "great tears rolled down the hardy old mariner's checks *[sic]* as he sadly admitted there was no hope of saving the 'good old ship.'"

In the end, both captains shared the blame as per this brief mention in the May 12, 1909 issue of the *Harwich Independent*: "The U.S. board of inspectors have reported on the recent collision between the steamships *Horatio Hall* and *H.F. Dimock* in Pollock Rip, and found Capt. John A. Thompson of the *Dimock* and Capt. W. Frank Jewell of the *Hall* equally responsible for the accident, and suspended the licenses of both captains for a period of 15 days."

■ ■ ■

Longfellow

The former excursion vessel *Longfellow* was later converted to a cargo ship, plying the waters of the northeast coast. In September of 1904, the 400-ton ship was carrying a dangerous cargo along the outer Cape coast when she met up with a storm. Though the crew was able to launch a boat and escape the ship, the *Longfellow* eventually sank, as reported in the *Barnstable Patriot*:

"The steamer *Longfellow*, which years ago ran between Provincetown and Boston, sprang a leak and sank three miles southeast of Highland Light, Friday night. She was loaded with 300 tons of dynamite and bound from Wilmington, Del., for Lake Superior. The crew of 16 men took to their boats, and landed through the assistance of the crews of the Highland and Peaked Hill Bar Stations. It seems strange that the *Longfellow* should be lost so near her home port." *Barnstable Patriot*, September 12, 1904.

A newspaper description of the shipwreck provided a word picture of what lifesavers were up against in their attempts to bring a wrecked crew ashore: "...the dynamite laden steamer *Longfellow* foundered off shore. Although the night was not bad, still the breakers were running high, and it was a trying time ... to attempt to launch the life-boat meant perhaps the sacrifice of the crew, and not to launch it might mean death to those on board the ill-fated steamer. It was a night that called for judgment, and on that judgment hung human life. It is questions like these, that strain men's nerves ..." *Harwich Independent*, March 8, 1905.

■

Yet, the tale of the *Longfellow* was not over, as two months later a storm visited these outermost shores, causing the wreck of the sunken vessel to stir in her undersea grave:

"The report of the explosion on Sunday night week, when the cargo of the steamer *Longfellow*, recently sunk off Truro, blew up, was plainly heard in this section. The life saving crews along the shores of the Cape at first thought an earthquake had taken place. They were only a few miles away and the force of the explosion was so great that the life saving stations were shaken until it seemed as if they would topple over." *Barnstable Patriot*, November 21, 1904.

■ ■ ■

Castagna

The winter of 1914 found the Italian bark *Castagna* off the coast of Wellfleet, iced up and in dire straits. She eventually wrecked and her crewmen were forced to climb into the rigging to avoid being swept overboard into the chilling sea. Eight of the crewmen were saved by lifesavers, although the Italian ship saw "the loss of her captain and four of the crew." The vessel itself "was torn to pieces Saturday by a northeast gale and scattered along the beach for many miles." As for the survivors, they were reported "very comfortable at Carney hospital Boston," although physicians initially "thought that the limbs of several of the patients would have to be amputated." *Harwich Independent*, February 23, 1914.

The newspaper article continued, mentioning, "Life-savers succeeded in rescuing the captain's chest containing the ship's papers and $7,000 in drafts as well as other valuables. All the nautical instruments, sails and some of the rigging were also brought ashore ..." Also, "On the body of one of the seamen who was frozen in the rigging was found $130 which was sent to the Italian consul in Boston." The bodies were buried and in time, life along the coast of Wellfleet returned to normal, with the name of *Castagna* now etched onto the roll of shipwrecked vessels that came to woe along the outermost shoreline of the Cape.

■

Yet, the tale of the *Castagna* was ongoing, as the following chapter written more than a week later and a number of miles away will attest: "The body of a young man believed to be that of the cabin boy of the bark *Castagna*, which was wrecked off the wireless station at Wellfleet, Feb 17, was picked up near the Old Harbor station, Chatham, Tuesday, ten miles up the beach from the disaster." Still a year later the body of Captain Gavi was found near the entrance to Nauset Harbor. It was almost perfectly preserved and still frozen solid. *Mooncussers of Cape Cod* by Henry Kittredge, page 79. *Harwich Independent*, March 4, 1914.

■ ■ ■

And this story of a vessel that had a collision with a bridge:

Belfast

By the spring of 1919, the Cape Cod Canal had seen five years of operation and thus five years of vessels successfully navigating its winding length. Granted, the canal in those early days was not nearly as wide, nor as deep, as it is today. And the drawbridges of that era which spanned her breadth were quite a bit smaller than the bridges of today. But still, the waterway was quite passable.

Unfortunately, that would not be the case for the 320-foot steamer *Belfast* during her first run through the canal in April 1919 as documented in this local newspaper report, bearing the telltale headline: "Steamer Hits Bridge."

"The steamer *Belfast* of the Eastern Steamship line on its first eastbound trip through the canal Wednesday morning broke her steering gear when approaching the Sagamore bridge in the Cape Cod canal, missed the open draw and crashed under the structure. The prow of the steamer passed under the lower beams of the bridge ... the pilot house and about 20 feet of the deckhouse were smashed into kindling wood."

According to the newspaper account, "There were about 100 passengers on the trip. The most of them were taken off by the canal tugs and landed at Sandwich." Yet there were some harrowing episodes that took place at the moment of impact. "A woman and her son were occupying one of the forward staterooms and they miraculously escaped serious injury, although sustaining a few cuts and bruises." Meanwhile, a man occupying the adjoining stateroom, who was sleeping at the time, was "quite badly injured," sustaining broken ribs.

"Work was begun at once by the crew to clear away the wreckage, which was done with axes, saws and acetylene torches for cutting the iron plates." But with the *Belfast* firmly wedged underneath, the drawbridge could not be closed throughout the entire day, and therefore no automobile traffic could cross to the woe of travelers. Finally, later that evening, with the assistance of three tugboats, the *Belfast* was pulled clear of the bridge and towed up to Boston. As for the bridge itself, it suffered "very little damage by the collision," although some of her girders were twisted by the impact. *Barnstable Patriot*, April 21, 1919.

■

Yet, the *Belfast's* collision with the Sagamore Bridge was not her first accident. Nearly five years earlier, the steamer rammed a vessel, and sent her to the bottom, as documented by the following from the October 10, 1914 issue of the *Evening Ledger – Philadelphia*: "The four-masted schooner *Alma N. A. Holmes*, from Philadelphia, was sunk off the Graves' Light early today in a dense fog by the inbound steamship *Belfast*, of the Bangor division of the Eastern Steamship Corporation. All hands of the schooner were saved." The accident was also covered by the *New York Times* on October 11, noting that the collision took place "off Marblehead about sunrise ... crew of the schooner escaped with difficulty, several of them being in their bunks when the crash came."

■

As for the fate of the *Belfast*, it is believed she was converted to a US troop transport ship and foundered off Washington State in 1947. www.hazegray.org; www.shipbuildinghistory.com; www.funbeach.com.

CHAPTER 5
Accidents, Miscues, and Thin Ice

"Trust not one night's ice," was the advice of a seventeenth century philosopher. Apparently, a lot of Cape Codders should have taken counsel to be wary of even five or six nights' ice. During a number of winters from Cape Cod's past, the population of local towns was decreased of people – and of a few horses and even deer – all victims of thin ice. Nor was there safety in climbing upwards either, as evidenced in tales of stunt flyers, flagpole painters, and telephone workers who suffered the effects of gravity while operating high above the ground.

■ ■ ■

As they say, all is well that ends well. It seems a three-year old Hyannis boy – the son of a Mr. Charles Berry – managed to fall into a well near which he had been playing. A twelve-year-old boy – the son of Captain Christopher Crowell – happened to be nearby and attempted to save the little boy. His efforts were in vain, but fortunately Jabez Baxter was passing by at the time and was alerted to the situation. Mr. Baxter was able to bring the boy out of the well. Though the child was described as "in an insensible condition," the boy is "now doing well" according to a January 4, 1870 *Barnstable Patriot* article.

■ ■ ■

"Mr. Isaiah Fish had a narrow escape from what might have been a serious accident. He was standing on a load of wood putting on his coat, his horse started suddenly and threw him off, bruising him, but breaking no bones." *Barnstable Patriot*, August 10, 1880.

■ ■ ■

Harvesting ice at local ponds was a necessary winter activity for many men in villages around the Cape. Blocks were cut by handsaw or by machine and then brought to shore where they were placed in a nearby icehouse. For instance, as reported in the February 27, 1894 issue of the *Hyannis Patriot*, at Sandwich E.T. Pope and his son "took advantage of Saturday's cold snap and commenced to cut ice in the morning." The ice thickness was about half a foot. "A large gang was later put to work and by midnight the older or main portion of the house was nearly filled." Some three decades later, Cape men were still harvesting ice, as the *Hyannis Patriot* reported on February 9, 1928 that "a crew of ice cutters have been harvesting the ice and filling the ice-house at Joshua's Pond, in Osterville, by moonlight, augmented by electric lights..."

Ice harvesting could be dangerous work, for one wrong step on thin ice could put a person in jeopardy. Such was the case in Dennis in 1908 with David Love, who "while helping to fill the Nobscusset ice-house, walked on thin ice and fell in." Fortunately, Love was plucked from the icy waters by Ben Eldridge and Clarence Sears. *Hyannis Patriot*, February 10, 1908.

In 1917, Seth H. Howes of West Chatham was not so lucky. While harvesting ice on White Pond around 5:45 p.m. with his brother-in-law, Freeman Ellis, Howes slipped and fell in. In an attempt to save him, Ellis also ended up in the water, holding onto the icy edge and calling out for help. Eventually he was saved by two men – N. Byron Small and George C. Cahoon – who heard his cries. Later, Howes' body "was recovered and taken to his home, where he had but a few minutes before partaken of his supper and departed for a little more daily toil" *Hyannis Patriot*, February 19, 1917.

■ ■ ■

The ice at Bumpus Pond, at Buzzards Bay, thickened to about six and a half inches in February of 1892, thick enough to create "a lively scene of ice men; six different gangs of from 11 to 15 men in each gang harvesting the article which keeps our butter cool in summer...some ploughing, some sawing, some carting, and as three of the houses are situated near the pond, a shute from pond to house is arranged, and it is pulled in by horse power." But a horse on ice can cause problems, and later in the afternoon a horse belonging to

Ice House at Auction.

Will be sold by Public Auction on MONDAY, the second day of December next, at 2 o'clock, p.m., on the prem
ises, the Ice House located near the south-west part of
Dennis Pond, with all the fixtures thereunto belonging.
                                    CHARLES THACHER; Auct'r.
    Yarmouth, Nov. 22.

Yarmouth Register, November 22, 1867

D. H. Baker of Monument Beach fell through the ice. "In crossing ploughed ice the animal being heavy broke through. He was finally rescued with no little work from his cold bath and driven home, after a good rubbing down." *Barnstable Patriot*, February 23, 1892.

Another horse fell through thin ice on a winter's day around the turn of the century, at Cotuit, as documented in the January 8, 1900 issue of the *Barnstable Patriot*: "Mr. James Brackett unfortunately had a horse break through the ice on Lewis Bay on the 2nd. He was plowing for Mr. Goodspeed and got on thin ice. He was rescued with much difficulty."

■ ■ ■

Meanwhile, at Sandwich, "Miss Nellie Kelleher met with an accident Saturday evening, while watching the process of filling the ice-house." It appears she did not watch her step and tumbled into a trench near the edge of the pond, sustaining "a number of severe bruises, though fortunately no bones were broken." *Hyannis Patriot*, February 27, 1894.

■ ■ ■

Beyond those stories of ice harvesters and their horses falling through the ice of frozen ponds, there are plenty of tales of everyday citizens doing the same. For instance, here's a report from the local paper of a man who, while fishing, fell through the ice and was fortunately rescued. "On Friday as George Bastien was on a fishing expedition at Mary Dunn's pond he chanced to step on some thin ice and was immediately precipitated into the icy water, just catching the firm ice by his elbows ... he was discovered by Joseph H. Maher and Chas. Perry who chanced to go to the pond with a load of material for the Maher ice house." Using a plank, the two men were able to extricate Bastien, and he was soon transported by ambulance to the new Cape Cod Hospital where "he was revived from his numbed condition." *Hyannis Patriot*, February 5, 1923.

"While skating on Turtle Pond" in the town of Wellfleet during the winter of 1908, "... Miss Lillian Howland fell in a spring hole and was barely rescued by Mr. Ernest and Master Atkins Berrio." As one can see by reading this short report, it was clearly an earlier and more elegant age when the characters involved were referred to as "Miss," "Mr.," and "Master." *Hyannis Patriot*, January 27, 1908.

Sometimes, the outcome was not a positive one, as depicted in this short mention under the headline "Two Drowned at Woods Hole" in the February 8, 1909 issue of the *Hyannis Patriot*: "While skating on a pond in a cedar swamp near Woods Hole Sunday afternoon, Charles Gottnebsen, wireless operator on the revenue cutter *Acushnet*, broke through the ice and both he and Seaman Oscar Rongved, also of the *Acushnet*, who made a brave attempt to rescue him, were drowned."

■ ■ ■

There also are numerous instances of children falling through the thin ice of Cape Cod ponds and lakes, some while skating, or sledding, or others while merely crossing the frozen body of water on their way home from school. Here are some instances from the 19th century, pulled from the pages of the Hyannis and Barnstable papers.

The first story comes from the winter of 1861, when two boys, "the sons of Mr. Wm. Robbins of East Harwich, aged 11 and 9 years," fell through the ice of a pond they were crossing. Their father "vigorously commenced breaking the ice toward them" in an effort to reach his sons. "In the mean time, Capt. George T. Pierce arrived at the scene of peril, plunged in, and brought out one boy after the other to their father." The two frozen boys, the older of which was not breathing, were taken to a nearby home where "family and neighbors rendered every assistance in their power." The older boy was revived and "both are now quite well." Captain Pierce, who it was noted "has rescued three persons from drowning during the past two years," received praise for his heroics and "deserves the life-long gratitude of the boys" according to the newspaper article, which concluded with the warning that "all youth to be careful when upon the ice." *Barnstable Patriot*, January 7, 1861.

Approaching winter of the very next year, the daughter of Chatham sea captain Philip Stetson was crossing Oyster Pond, while coming home from school, when she fell through the ice. Using a boat to reach her, two local men and a local woman – a Mr. Levi Atwood and Mr. and Mrs. Rufus Emery, "all got into deep water in their efforts to release the child." Their efforts were successful, as the paper reported, "The little girl is now as well as ever." The same issue of the paper made mention of "two Misses, a daughter of Dr. Brownell and the other of Rev. Mr. Willett," who also fell through the ice of a local pond on the very same day. Apparently these two girls were skating at the time, and were luckily seen by Mr. Gideon Eldridge, Jr. "who was providentially near" and came to the rescue. *Barnstable Patriot*, December 23, 1862.

Some years later, in the winter of 1894, two Sandwich children "belonging to Mrs. Eunice Tinkham narrowly escaped drowning in the Mill pond Monday afternoon, in the vicinity of the Braiding Works." The twelve-year-old sister was pushing a sled that held her younger brother across the ice, "and carelessly ventured upon a thin place and both broke through." Their mother, who watched the ordeal from the shore was unable to reach them. Somehow, the girl was able to get her little brother out of the water and onto the solid ice. She then hung on to the edge of the ice until assistance arrived in the form of a Mr. A. R. Pope and a Mr. Josiah Newcomb, who used a ladder to rescue the girl. Picked up from the *Sandwich Observer* newspaper by the *Hyannis Patriot*, February 27, 1894.

■ ■ ■

In the winter of 1928, a deer found itself on thin ice. According to the report of a Hyannis man named Chester Jordan, who was traveling through Waquoit on his way home from Falmouth, "His attention was attracted to two men in a boat trying to rescue a deer in the water. The deer could not get to shore on account of the ice. The men worked hard and finally saved the deer." The deer, once on solid ground, was "away in a flash." The article concluded in philosophical fashion: "Who will say that these men were not better sportsmen than the ones who will kill the same deer perhaps next fall?" *Hyannis Patriot*, February 9, 1928.

■ ■ ■

In his book, *The Outermost House*, author/naturalist Henry Beston described a similar situation with a deer in winter that had wandered into the Nauset marsh channel nearby his Fo'castle home. She sought refuge on a small island that was subject to the tides, and remained there throughout the day and throughout the bitter cold night. Beston wrote, "I have often paused to wonder how that delicate and lovely creature endured so cruel a night, how she survived the slow rise of the icy tide about her poor legs..." The next morning, she was rescued by a crew from the nearby Nauset Coast Guard station. "All the Nauset crew had taken an interest. Catching sight of the poor creature fighting for life in the drift, three of the men put off in a skiff, poled the ice away with their oars, and shepherded the doe ashore." Though weak from her ordeal, and falling repeatedly to the ground, she eventually "stood up and stayed up, and walked off into the pines." *The Outermost House*, by Henry Beston, 1928, pgs 78-80.

■ ■ ■

"International steeplejack" Gardie Watt of Edinburgh, Scotland was in Barnstable in September of 1928 painting the 135-foot high flagpole outside the courthouse, along with fellow steeplejack Hain Bask of Providence, Rhode Island. Watt was a World War I hero who flew for the Royal Scottish Airship Corps, and was wounded "in air maneuvers" in Northern France. Later, after the war, he journeyed to Hollywood to try his hand as a stunt flyer, but was further injured, eventually forcing him out of the stunt business. Since he had no fear of heights, he picked up work as a steeplejack, painting church steeples, flagpoles, stacks, and other objects situated well off the ground. According to the news report, "Jack's nerves are as good as ever." *Hyannis Patriot*, September 13, 1928.

■ ■ ■

Another man who made his living high above the ground was Theodore Chaffin, of the Buzzards Bay Electric Company. On Saturday evening, June 16, 1917 he was severely injured when he fell twenty feet from a pole he was working on at Woods Hole. "It is thought that he lost his balance and in trying to save himself from falling, clutched at the electric light wire, receiving a severe shock. He was taken to St. Luke's hospital, New Bedford, where he is dangerously ill." *Hyannis Patriot*, June 25, 1917.

Further research provides a happy ending to the story. A brief mention in the July 16, 1917 issue of the *Hyannis Patriot* stated that Chaffin "is much improved and expects to leave St. Luke's hospital, New Bedford, in a few days." The Dec 10 issue provided an update: "Theodore Chaffin has recently returned from New Hampshire where he has been several months for the benefit of his health and has resumed work for the Buzzards Bay Electric Company, being stationed here [in Hyannis] for the present." Later, now working for the Cape & Vineyard Electric Company, he made Hyannis his home, as the *Barnstable Patriot* reported on December 13, 1920, moving "his family from Falmouth to this place ... a more central location for his business."

■ ■ ■

A near miss along the railroad tracks led to the following editorial: "During the past week two inmates of the Barnstable House of Correction missed death by inches when their tractor was hit by a train on the county farm crossing. The tractor was a total loss but the men were, by some miracle saved. This incident brings to mind the fact that the numerous railroad crossings on the Cape without flashing red signals are still spots to Stop, Look and Listen. Because there is no longer year-round passenger service to the Cape, people have become less cautious in their crossing habits. The railroad has become slovenly in its upkeep of the roadbeds and brush now obscures the motorists's view down the tracks on many crossings. Freights still roll through, summertime passenger trains still use these tracks. Since this is the case – we are not dealing with an abandoned line – the railroad should be forced to keep all crossings and the surrounding area in a safer condition than they now do." *Barnstable Patriot*, July 26, 1962.

■ ■ ■

Sometimes, the "deer in the headlights" could actually be the "man in the cranberry bog." The deer report of one particular week in 1914 included the bagging of more than a dozen deer ... and one cranberry worker. "The shooting of 13 deer in Barnstable Co. was reported up to Friday night ... Seth Bowman of West Falmouth shot a deer last week. It was a five-year-old buck and weighed about 185 pounds ... Clayton Peters a cranberry bog worker in East Wareham was shot and seriously wounded last Tuesday supposedly mistaken for a deer." *Barnstable Patriot*, November 23, 1914.

■ ■ ■

On a summer morning in 1961, drivers were surprised to see a large elephant at the Route 6 rotary circle in West Barnstable. On its way to setting up in Harwich, a Mills Brothers' three ring circus truck had overturned. "Little Burma," one of the featured animals in the circus was coaxed into pulling the truck upright. Commuters were delayed about twenty minutes while the recovery effort took place, no doubt wondering how believable the excuse "I was held up by an elephant," would be received at work. *Barnstable Patriot*, July 30, 1961.

Melancholy Accident.—We have just learned that a melancholy and fatal accident occurred in Sandwich woods yesterday. Two different parties were out hunting deer—one from Carver, the other from Wareham—and a dog of one of the parties having started a deer, Mr Augustus Holmes of the Wareham party having no knowledge that any other hunters were in the woods, and discovering what he thought to be a deer, some distance ahead in the bushes, fired, and killed instantly Mr Jerome Purrington, of Carver. So deadly was the shot, that Mr P. never spoke, or moved, after Mr Holmes fired. Mr P. was about 22 years of age, of good character, and his loss will be much lamented by relatives and friends.

It may be well to remark, that in the extensive woods in and about Sandwich and Wareham accidents of this nature are frequently occurring.—Our informant, who has been occasionally engaged in these sports, tells us that he has been struck at three different times by shots from sportsmen. These facts should warn strangers and others frequenting this forest, to guard against similar accidents by giving some signal of their presence.—*Patriot.*

Hunting tragedies were not unusual in the nineteenth century as this accidental shooting in the woods of Sandwich indicates.
From the *Yarmouth Register,* August 7, 1845

CHAPTER 6
Crime & Punishment

Someone once said that laws were made to be broken. The more laws, the more opportunity for transgressions. From the colonial times to the modern era, Cape Codders have always had trouble with rules. Here are some of the transgressions and some of the consequences.

■ ■ ■

17th Century

In the early days of Plymouth, before the first Thanksgiving, it seems there was a disagreement between at least two members of the original *Mayflower* Pilgrims. Edward Dotey and Edward Leister, both in their early twenties at the time, and both being servants of Pilgrim Stephen Hopkins, fought "the first and last duel" in Plymouth Colony, according to the book *Saints and Strangers*, by George Willison. As printed in the September 2000 issue of *"The Mayflower Quarterly,"* the two Edwards "were arraigned on June 18, 1621 before the company for trial, because they had fought a duel with sword and dagger in which both were wounded. They were sentenced to have their heads and feet tied together for twenty-four hours without food or drink." The sentence was later commuted to just one hour with the promise that they would behave themselves.

■ ■ ■

In the days of the Plymouth Colony, men were proscribed from wearing long hair. A law barring hair below the ears was passed in 1649 which declared: "Forsomuch as the wearing of long hair, after the manner of the Russians and barbarous Indians, has begun to invade New England, contrary to the rule of God's word, and the commendable custom of all the Godly, . . . We the magistrates, who have subscribed this paper, do declare and manifest our dislike and detestation against the wearing of such long hair, as against a thing uncivil and unmanly, whereby men do deform themselves, and offend sober and modest men and do corrupt good manners." *History of Cape Cod*, by Frederick Freeman, Volume I, page 179.

■ ■ ■

Richard Berry, a seventeenth century settler of Bass River, was fined five shillings at the March 1659 Plymouth court session for ignoring the exhortations of the preacher during worship service in Yarmouth. His crime was compounded by the fact that he and four other men removed themselves from the meeting house "during time of exercise," and indulged in smoking tobacco. *Genealogical Notes of Barnstable Families*, by Amos Otis, 1979 edition, page 122.

■ ■ ■

In March of 1660, Ralph Smith of Eastham was charged with "unjustly appropriating to his own use a fish belonging to said town." The "fish" was undoubtedly a whale and the court ruled that Smith had to return it to its rightful owners, "...be they English or Indians." He was fined 40 shillings for his transgression and had to pay court costs of 1 pound, 14 shillings, and 6 cents. *Records of the Plymouth Colony: Judicial Acts 1636-1692*, 1877 Edition, printed by the press of William White, Boston, page 99.

■ ■ ■

Elizabeth Snow, wife of James Snow of Eastham, was fined ten shillings on March 5, 1684, for "using railing expressions on the Lord's Day to the Reverend Samuel Treat." *Records of the Plymouth Colony: Court Orders: 1678-1694*, 1856 Edition, printed by the press of William White, Boston, page 152.

■ ■ ■

18th Century

The last female to be executed in Massachusetts was a Cape-born woman. Bathsheba Ruggles was born in Sandwich in 1746, the daughter of Timothy Ruggles and Bathsheba Bourne. She married Joshua Spooner in 1766 and moved with him to Brookfield, Massachusetts. During the Revolution, she became involved with a young soldier named Ezra Ross and became pregnant by him. To get rid of her hus-

JIM COOGAN PHOTO

Typical Colonial stocks. Outside the Dan'l Webster Inn, Sandwich.

band, she hired two deserters from the British army and together, with Ross, the conspirators drowned the unsuspecting spouse.

The foursome was arrested quickly and held for trial and eventually found guilty of murder in Worcester. While there was no doubt as to Bathsheba's guilt in the affair, the issue of her pregnancy troubled the court. Could they execute a pregnant woman? Several times her execution was put off as judges tried to decide what to do. Finally in July of 1778, Bathsheba Spooner went to the hangman in front of an enormous crowd – many of whom were still not sure that taking the life of a pregnant woman was morally correct. "The Case of Bathsheba Spooner," in *American Antiquarian Society Proceedings*, Vol 5, October 1888, page 430.

■ ■ ■

19th Century

The "Come Outers," a nineteenth century Pentecostal protestant religious sect, often disrupted services in the more orthodox churches on the Cape. The group held that the old traditional denominations had strayed from the true message of Christianity and they were vocal in condemning what they saw as idolatry and "wicked practices."

On Christmas Eve, 1842, when the Reverend George Stearns of the Barnstable Methodist Church asked for prayers from the congregation, William Loring prayed that "the temple might not be polluted." Mrs. Charlotte Smith, a stranger seated at the rear of the church, stood up and shouted at him. "It is already polluted!" Ignoring the outburst, the choir began singing Christmas carols. Mrs. Smith attempted to shout over them. "It is the Devil's song and the Devil is singing it!"

Later, when Benjamin Baker offered a prayer, Mrs. Smith called him a Pharisee and a hypocrite. The authorities arrested her and she was charged with disturbing public worship. At the spring session of the Court of Common Pleas, Charlotte Smith was found guilty and fined $3.00 plus court costs. She refused to pay and demanded to be put in jail. Instead, her father paid the fine and the matter was forgotten. *Yarmouth Register*, April 6, 1843.

■ ■ ■

Most people associate the punishment of tar and feathering with the Revolutionary War period. But in at least one instance, the practice was still being done on Cape Cod as late as the 1850's. James Hughes of Wellfleet was grabbed out of a cooper's shop on the evening of December 29, 1855. Seven young men were later accused of tarring and feathering Mr. Hughes. They also took his watch and $200 that he was carrying. All seven men were held without bail in the County Jail and their trial was scheduled for the April session of the court of Common Pleas. *Yarmouth Register*, January 11, 1856.

■ ■ ■

A Wampanoag tribal member named Oliver Jones was arrested in Mashpee for "unlawfully opening a letter belonging to Lisbon Johnson on the 9th of August [1864] with the design of prying into the secrets of said Johnson." He was taken to Boston and arraigned and later found guilty before Judge Hallett. *Yarmouth Register*, November 18, 1864.

■ ■ ■

The novel *Cape Cod Folks*, written by Sally Pratt McLean and published in 1881, was the first American work of fiction to be the subject of a libel suit in the United States. Mr. Lorenzo L. Nightingale of Cedarville sued the publisher, Alex Williams, in Plymouth District Court for "libelous statements" made about him in the book. Nightingale claimed that the story vilified him and brought him into "hatred, contempt, and ridicule." The author maintained that the novel was not intended as a description of Nightingale, but represented "a character more exalted than the plaintiff possesses." Nightingale asked for $10,000 but the jury decided that the "injury" was worth only $1,095.00 – still, a considerable sum in the late 19th century. Subsequent editions of the book, which was a best seller, changed Nightingale's name to Benney Leonard. *The Cape Cod Bee*, February 22, 1884.

■ ■ ■

20th Century

In the year 1903 there was a warrant on the Harwich town meeting agenda: "Article 77: To see if the town will vote to raise the sum of fifty dollars for the suppression of crime." From Harwich town records.

■ ■ ■

Times were certainly tough when even cranberries weren't safe. Such was the case back in the early 20th century as mentioned in the November 21, 1904 issue of the *Barnstable Patriot*, as reported by the paper's Sandwich correspondent: "District Police Officer Bradford of Hyannis is looking after the thieves who broke into the storehouse of Capt. 'Nat' Swift of Cedarville on Monday night and stole ten barrels of choice cranberries. Officer Bradford is a hard worker and is determined to catch the thieves unless they leave this part of the country."

■ ■ ■

Edwin White of Yarmouth was fined $75.00 in Plymouth District Court in September of 1906 for harvesting cranberries on the Lord's Day in Carver, Massachusetts. Judge Osborne held that this was not a "work of necessity" as defined by the law. *Barnstable Patriot*, September 26, 1904.

■ ■ ■

In his book about Provincetown, *Art in Narrow Streets*, Ross Moffett has a tale about the playwright Eugene O'Neill being arrested in the early days of World War I when authorities mistook O'Neill for a spy when he was seen carrying a black box into the dunes behind the town. According to Moffett, rumors had been circulating that someone was signaling German submarines off the coast. The "black box," said Moffett, was nothing more than a Corona typewriter that was being carried by the then obscure writer of one-act plays who simply wanted a quiet place to work.

Meanwhile, in their biography, *O'Neill*, by Arthur and Barbara Gelb, the authors say that O'Neill and a friend were arrested in March of 1917, a full month before the U.S. entered the war. Because O'Neill had made no secret of his pacifist beliefs, he was distrusted by some residents of the Cape tip. According to the Gelbs, O'Neill was arrested at the instigation of the chief of the wireless station in North Truro, who saw two men walking near the facility and believed they were German spies. O'Neill and his friend were held in the jail in the basement of the Provincetown town hall for a few hours and then released.

■ ■ ■

"Captain Perry's Jinx:" In the summer of 1918, tugboat Captain Joseph Perry came under fire from a German submarine off Nauset Beach. He survived that adventure. But six years later he found himself in hot water with federal authorities over an immigration issue. Perry had agreed to bring 29 Cape Verdean passengers to the United States in his schooner *Matthew S. Greer*. But just after sailing, a new restrictive law on immigration took effect. When he arrived in Boston, he could not unload his passengers.

As he waited for clarification about the status of the immigrants, Captain Perry had to pay for the immigrants' needs while they were housed aboard his vessel. After two months, he was told that he must return his passengers back to Cape Verde. But the night before he was scheduled to sail, they all escaped and were never caught. Captain Perry was fined $43,000 on the ground that he did not take all necessary precautions to prevent their escape. *Yarmouth Register*, November 29, 1924.

■ ■ ■

The first and only person from Cape Cod to be electrocuted for the crime of murder was Sylvester N. Fernandes of Mashpee. He went to the chair on August 11, 1932 after being convicted of killing John Alves of West Barnstable the previous December. *Barnstable Patriot*, August 18, 1932.

■ ■ ■

The 1936 annual town meeting warrant for the town of Truro contained an article supporting "strict censorship of bathing suits in the more public places." From Truro town records.

■ ■ ■

The 1939 Provincetown town warrant had an article that probably would not be there today. It proposed the banning of shorts in any public area of the town except the beaches. "No person over 10 years of age, shall appear in any public place, except a bathing beach, in a bathing suit, shorts, halter, or immodest dress, unless covered by an overcoat or wrap coming at least to the knees. However, the foregoing shall not apply to Boy Scouts or any athletic contest." The article was passed at the annual town meeting by a narrow vote and was criticized by a number of weekly newspapers as an unwanted form of censorship. From the Provincetown Town Report for 1939.

■ ■ ■

"Apprehension of an Enemy Alien." So read the front-page headline of the May 2, 1944 *Cape Cod Standard Times*. The enemy alien turned out to be a 50-year-old baker by the name of Paul Knoblauch who lived on Barnstable Road in Hyannis. Knoblauch, who was born in Blongweiz, Germany, had come to the Cape in 1941 to take a job in a Hyannis pastry shop. His arrest came when Barnstable police learned that he possessed a .22 caliber rifle, a weapon for which he did not have a permit. Claiming that he was using the rifle to shoot rats on his property, Knoblauch was nevertheless held for a few days before an investigation by the U.S. Attorney's office in Boston figured out that he was no threat to the security of the nation and he was released.

■ ■ ■

In 1977 while making a nighttime delivery, a man driving a truck filled with a load of marijuana got the vehicle firmly stuck under the Scraggy Neck railroad bridge in Cataumet. When morning came, police had no difficulty rounding up the culprit. *Cape Cod Railroads*, by Robert Farson, page 184.

☞ Petitions signed by Messrs. Jos. O. Procter and 2325 others of Gloucester; of Abijah Mayo and 119 others of Eastham : of Elisha Snow, Jr., and 205 others of Harwich ; of Geo. Shove and 140 others of Yarmouth ; of Isaac Green and others of Truro, and Henry Kelley and others of Harwich ; H. H. Sears and others of Dennis, and Josiah Freeman and others of Orleans, protesting against the proposed law against weir and seine fishing, were presented in the Mass House of Representatives last week.

Fiercely independent, Cape Codders resisted any laws they felt compromised their freedom. From the *Yarmouth Register*, February 25, 1870.

CHAPTER 7
A Little Religion

Religion influenced the settlement pattern of Cape Cod. From the Pilgrims, Quakers, Methodists, and "Come Outers," to Unitarians, Christian Scientists, Catholics, and Jews, spiritual fervor has raised up a peninsula full of interesting individuals and related stories.

■ ■ ■

In the colonial period, it was common for church members to own their own pews. The sale of the pews helped support the church and echoed social stratification as the wealthiest people purchased the choicest seats. Pews were subject to probate and were sold like any other real property. In the Barnstable County Registry of Deeds there is a record of one such transaction. On September 15, 1817, Winthrop Sears of Yarmouth sold "a one half interest in a pew in the South Yarmouth meeting house owned in common with Zenas Crowell." The deed states that the pew was "bounded on the North by seats reserved, on the East by the pew of Richard Sears and others, on the South by Timothy Crowell's pew, and on the West by the broad aisle."

■ ■ ■

In the first years of the nineteenth century, Sandwich, like many Cape Cod towns, was involved in a religious controversy. A rift developed in the Congregational Church that split the membership between liberals who challenged the older orthodox forms of worship and conservatives who wanted to keep things as they were. At a general parish meeting in 1811, the liberals voted to remove the Reverend Jonathan Burr as pastor. Burr left with about a hundred members of the congregation and formed a new assembly of worshipers – the Calvinistic Congregational Church.

Burr and his followers built a new house of worship on Water Street just down the street from the old church. This did not satisfy everyone. The next door neighbor to the new building was Melatiah Bourne who had been one of the people behind the ouster of Reverend Burr. To show his displeasure at having Burr's congregation right next door, Bourne built a barn as close as he could to the new building and made sure the open end faced it. During services, Bourne regularly stirred up his animals – some of which were pigs, so the sounds and smells wafted into the adjacent church building. His so-called "spite barn" eventually ended up across the street from Sandwich town hall and is now attached to the Sandwich Glass Museum complex. "History of the Original Congregational Church in Sandwich," from a series of articles published in the *Yarmouth Register*, May 5 & August 11, 1877.

■ ■ ■

Typical of early Cape Cod ministers was the Reverend Daniel Johnson who was the pastor of the Orleans Congregational Church from 1808 to 1820. A graduate of Brown University, Reverend Johnson married 244 couples. Among them were 17 sea captains. He held a number of religious revivals, took in 150 new members, baptized 525 people, and officiated at the burials of numerous sailors who were drowned or lost at sea. For this work, Reverend Johnson received a salary of $600 a year and his own pew. From the records of the Orleans Congregational Church as compiled by Ruth L. Barnard.

■ ■ ■

In the chancel of the "Christopher Wren" church in Sandwich is a small bell that some claim is the oldest bell in America. Its origins stem from a shipwreck that happened off the Sandwich coast in the winter of 1702/1703. The ill-fated crewmembers of the vessel were all New Yorkers bound for Boston. The citizens of Sandwich gathered the bodies from the beach and gave them a decent burial in the cemetery behind the town hall on Grove Street. The captain, Peter Adolph, rated a special stone that is still in the old burial ground off Grove Street.

The wife of the dead captain, grateful for the actions of the people of Sandwich, sent the town a bell cast in Munich, Germany in 1675. It hung in the Congregational Church until a new church was built in 1756. Because it was considered too small, the old bell was sold and wound up as the bell for the County Courthouse in Barnstable.

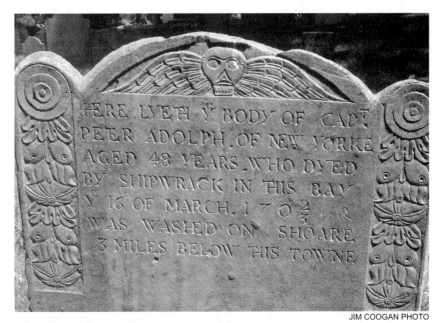

JIM COOGAN PHOTO

The grave marker of Captain Peter Adolph.

When a fire destroyed that building in 1827, the bell was put into the new courthouse until 1872, when, on July 4th of that year, some local youths damaged it by hitting it with a hammer.

The damaged bell was taken down and put on exhibit in the courthouse lobby until 1963 when it returned to Sandwich where it now sits in a revered spot in the foyer of the First Church of Christ, not more than a couple of miles from the site of the shipwreck disaster. The bell is fourteen inches high and about the same in diameter at the bottom. Running around the rim is a scroll which bears the date, 1675, and the motto in Latin: "If God be for us, who can be against us?" From a brochure published by the Sandwich Historical Society in 1967.

■ ■ ■

Sagamore Beach was, at one time, home to the Christian Endeavor Colony where summer "Sociological Congresses" were held. Described as "a place of spiritual unity," the colony brought together a wide variety of prominent business and religious leaders in the early 20th century for discussions about the social problems of the day. *Cape Cod Magazine*, August 1916.

■ ■ ■

The first religious service for Jews living on Cape Cod was held on Friday evening, November 3, 1933 at the Ocean Street home of Mrs. Annie S. Pearlstein in Hyannis. Rabbi Samson Shain officiated at the service. *Barnstable Patriot*, November 9, 1933.

■ ■ ■

The oldest working pipe organ in continuous use in the United States is located in the South Dennis Congregational Church. It was originally built in 1762 in London, England by the famous organ builder, John Snetzler. As the church grew to be the home of many wealthy sea captains, the instrument was brought to Dennis and installed in the church in 1854. The cost at the time was $460.00. "*A History of the Congregational Church of South Dennis,*" compiled by G. Kenneth Rogers, church historian, 1992.

■ ■ ■

The term "Bibleback" was a reference to Cape Cod fishermen who were reluctant to cast their nets on Sundays. Apparently the Wellfleet mackerel schooner *William Butler* had a crew of Biblebacks aboard. In a logbook of a voyage between August and November of 1860, fifteen successive Sundays went by without a mention that the vessel took even a single fish on the Sabbath. From the John Emory papers, William Brewster Nickerson Archives, Cape Cod Community College.

■ ■ ■

We usually associate a "necktie party" with quick old western justice. But at one time on Cape Cod, "necktie parties" were part of the social life of most villages. At church suppers, each single young lady made herself an apron, the brighter the color the better. She used the extra material to make a necktie, which was sealed in an envelope. Gentlemen paid a dollar, sight unseen, to buy an envelope. The church would use the money for missionary work. The gentleman would get to share supper with the girl whose apron matched the tie in the envelope. From an account of the history of the South Truro Meeting House, by Phyllis Duganne.

■ ■ ■

In 1820, the town of Brewster appointed a committee "to keep the meeting-house clear of dogs and to kill them if their owners will not keep them out," and compensation of $3.00 was voted therefore.

The 1810 Quaker meeting house in East Sandwich. Quakers were considered odd by their orthodox Sandwich neighbors when they arrived to establish a community in 1657. The building was pre-fabricated in Maine and shipped in pieces by schooner to Sandwich where it was unloaded and re-assembled by the members of the Quaker community.

Cape Cod: The Right Arm of Massachusetts: An Historical Narrative, by Charles F. Swift, page 270.

■ ■ ■

In the winter of 1936, a protest against an application to open a tavern in Harwich Port took on an interesting twist. The meeting was held at the Exchange Building in Harwich Center. A former pastor of the West Harwich Baptist church, Reverend David T. Richards, asked to be recognized. When he rose to speak, instead of a speech, he sang an original verse opposing the application to the tune of the Welsh national anthem. Following his unusual musical plea to deny the request, selectmen took the matter under advisement. Shortly after, the application was denied. *Yarmouth Register*, February 21, 1936.

West Harwich.

The Baptist society have commenced improving their church edifice, by raising it about 10 feet and fitting up a vestry and other convenient rooms underneath. The change will be a decided convenience and improvement to the appearance of the church.

—The ladies connected with the Baptist society gave a Fair and Concert on the evenings of Tuesday and Wednesday of last week. The variety of useful and fancy articles offered met a ready sale, and the Old Folks' Concert was a great attraction. Not the least of the pleasure of the occasion was derived from the fine singing of Messrs. J. S. Chase and W. B. Kelley. About $300 realized, which will go towards improving the church.

From the *Yarmouth Register*, February 25, 1870

CHAPTER 8

Earthquakes, Waterspouts, and Meteorites

Whether from deep within the bedrock of New England, from the ocean, or even from outer space, Cape Cod has experienced some very unusual natural phenomena. At one time these happenings were considered portents of some important future event. Today, science has taken away most of the romance associated with cyclones, earth tremors, and things that occasionally fall mysteriously from the sky.

■ ■ ■

One may not associate earthquakes with Cape Cod and the northeastern United States, but according to the website of the Northeast States Emergency Consortium (www.nesec.org) there have been some 2,400 earthquakes in the region since the time of the great earthquake of 1638, circa 6.5 magnitude, that Governor Bradford mentioned in his journal:

"This year, aboute ye 1. or 2. of June, was great & fearfull earthquake; it was in this place heard before it was felte. It came with a rumbling noyse, or low murmure, like unto remoate thunder; it came from ye norward, & passed southward. As ye noyse aproched nerer, they earth begane to shake, and came at length with that violence as caused platters, dishes, & such like things as stoode upon shelves, to clatter & fall downe." *Of Plimoth Plantation*, by William Bradford.

Bradford's journal entry continued: "How ever it was very terrible for ye time, and as ye men were set talking in ye house, some women & others were without ye dores, and ye earth shooke with yt violence as they could not stand without catching hould of ye posts & pails yt stood next them ; but ye violence lasted not long." The NESEC website lists the epicenter of this particular earthquake as somewhere in central New Hampshire based on other historical reports of the tremor felt throughout the northeast.

According to the NESEC, there were a brace of earthquakes "off Cape Cod" in November 1755, another in February 1766, one in August 1847, and another in October 1965. In March 1860, an earthquake was documented in the *Barnstable Patriot* as follows: "On Wednesday evening last, near ten o'clock, quite a severe shock of an earthquake was experienced in this vicinity; as well as in almost every other part of eastern Massachusetts...The shock was sensibly felt in almost every town on the Cape, and numerous persons who had retired were awakened from their sleep, and arose to find out the occasion of so strange a phenomenon." *Barnstable Patriot*, March 20, 1860.

In its April 27, 1869 issue, the *Barnstable Patriot* reported, "A slight shock of an earthquake was felt in some portions of Plymouth County last week." While the April 12, 1909 issue of the *Hyannis Patriot* mused, "Parts of Cape Cod are still wondering if that was a real earthquake quiver or only a joking jolt."

The year 1929 saw a "Slight Earthquake" according to the headline of a *Hyannis Patriot* report, with the subhead: "Cape Feels Tremors That Were Felt All Over New England." That slight earthquake "shook the eastern part of the United States and Canada for several minutes Monday afternoon" and "rocked many of the houses and buildings here, beginning at 3:36 p.m. and lasting for a minute or more." The article continued with: "The only known damage in Hyannis was cracked plaster in the east wall of the rear corridor of the town office building ... In many of the larger buildings the shock passed unnoticed ... In buildings where the shock was more pronounced, persons became aware of what was occurring when water in containers was spilled, and articles moved from their resting places." The newspaper also made mention of an earthquake five years earlier, and that this present shock, "although quite noticeable ... was not as much so as the one experienced several years ago." *Hyannis Patriot*, November 21, 1929.

The Harwich newspaper also commented on the same seismic activity: "The earthquake shock of Monday afternoon was heard and felt by many in this section, as throughout the State and New England. This new contribution of nature to the general variety of New England; resourceful weather disturbances, are becoming rather frequent for the nervously inclined." *Harwich Independent*, November 20, 1929.

Water-spout, from *The Waterworld* by J.W. Van DerVoot

■ ■ ■

The latter quarter of the 19th century saw a number of waterspouts visit Cape Cod as documented in the following newspaper reports.

"Barnstable and Yarmouth on Tuesday last were treated to a first class sensation in the shape of a WATERSPOUT. ... it was first seen about 1 o'clock, P.M., forming over Scorton, and travelling in a zig-zag course in a direction across Barnstable Harbor. A tunnel shaped projection – presenting the appearance of a balloon with its upper portion hidden – hanging from a huge black mass of vapor, was whirling, and gyrating and surging against the clear sky below, as though agitated by fierce internal commotions ... Sand, leaves, stones flew into the air, trees were uprooted, and a general panic among inanimate things resulted at once. Leaving the shore, it struck the water at the upper part of Barnstable harbor ... Crossing the harbor it struck the shore again, in Barnstable, passing through an orchard of the Widow Thos. Holmes, stripping the trees of fruit, leaves and twigs." *Barnstable Patriot*, August 23, 1870.

The article continued: "Keeping its crooked course, it struck a corner of Mr. Josiah Hinckley's lumber yard, scattering the piled lumber in every direction, and throwing it far out into the water." After causing some additional damage, sinking a sailboat and destroying a bathhouse, the cyclone "left the shore for the water, crossing the harbor, and finally breaking over the water, off Sandy Neck Lighthouse." Also documented in *Barnstable – Three Centuries of a Cape Cod Town*, by Donald G. Trayser, page 477.

Almost a year later another waterspout visited the Cape, this time along the south coast – "A Waterspout was seen in the Vineyard Sound, southwest from Hyannis about 2 o'clock Friday" – as reported in the *Barnstable Patriot* on June 20, 1871.

On June 29, 1880, "a genuine water spout" appeared in the vicinity of the Upper Cape. "Its origin is differently given by various observers, some locating it near Onset Bay, others over the water of Buzzard's Bay back of Monument Beach Islands, others still, in a cove between Sconticut Neck and Mattapoissett Neck. It finally struck the land near Barlow's landing in Pocassett, ripping up the sods from the bank, a foot thick and a yard square." The waterspout destroyed stonewalls, picked up a dory some fifty feet into the air (and then dropped it to the ground where it was "dashed to pieces"), and even briefly levitated a cow "belonging to Capt. William Barlow, happening to be in the line of its march," which was fortunately returned to the ground unharmed. The waterspout eventually petered out "before reaching the village of Pocassett ... and was drawn rapidly up into the cloud." During the weather event, hail "the size of cranberries" fell and there was one report of "hail stones as large as pigeons' eggs." *Barnstable Patriot*, August 3 and 10, 1880.

A West Dennis sea captain reported seeing waterspouts on his route up the east coast as documented in this article from the *Barnstable Patriot*: "Sch. *Sarah E. Ward*, Wixon (master), reports on Aug. 30, at mid-day, while on passage from Philadelphia to Boston, lat. 40 deg. 24 m., lon. 71 deg, 57 m., sighted eight waterspouts ... Capt. Wixon has followed the sea for twenty years and says these are the first waterspouts he ever saw in this latitude." Those coordinates would have placed the *Sarah E. Ward* and Captain Wixon several hundred miles southwest of Martha's Vineyard. *Barnstable Patriot*, September 13, 1887.

In the final years of the 19th century, a pair of water cyclones were witnessed off Martha's Vineyard as evidenced by this short mention in the September 7, 1896 issue of the *Barnstable Patriot*: "Two waterspouts were noticed, in the direction of Cottage City, about 1 p.m. on the 19th."

Meanwhile, Captain Edgar R. Taylor, who hailed from Boston, was sailing with a number of other people for Hyannis when they also saw waterspouts in the vicinity of Martha's Vineyard: "Among the objects of interest that claimed their attention were the waterspouts which occurred up the Vineyard Sound that day ... The clouds and the water seemed to be holding a consultation through the medium of a cylindrical column of black cloud, funnel shaped, small at the bottom, twisting and turning and wheeling the water high into the air ... There were three following each other at short intervals." *Harwich Independent*, September 1, 1896.

■ ■ ■

It seems that waterspouts and meteorites shared the skies in August 1880, as reported in the pages of the *Barnstable Patriot*: "On the day before the waterspout a South Wellfleet boy was out on a hill picking huckleberries, when he saw a 'ball of fire about as big as a bucket fall into the bay.' It fell about ten o'clock A.M., a mile from this boy, and was undoubtedly a meteorite." Apparently, the boy's father was a mariner who witnessed a similar meteorite fall into the ocean "about twenty feet astern" of the vessel on which he was sailing, "so near that the crew saw the splash and heard the hissing of the red hot mass." *Barnstable Patriot*, August 10, 1880.

"A beautiful meteor" fell within the view of Cape Cod residents in November 1895, as reported in the local newspaper. The meteorite, which was seen just after ten o'clock on a Saturday night, "was first seen in the north east and it travelled to the south west at quite a moderate rate leaving a fiery path of great extent." According to witnesses, "it was the largest and longest visible meteor we ever saw." *Barnstable Patriot*, November 18, 1895.

A meteorite falling off Truro made the news with a brief mention in the *Hyannis Patriot* in 1917: "What probably was a meteorite fell into the ocean within fifty feet of the fishing schooner *Thalia* about eighty miles east of Highland Light Wednesday, at dawn, and three members of the crew who were on deck watch got the scare of their lives." *Hyannis Patriot*, June 25, 1917.

In September 1923, Cummaquid resident Walter Marchant reported seeing "two distinct flashes" in the sky, "changing from a brilliant yellow to a bright blue ... followed by a noticeable tremor of the earth." This story was corroborated by a report issued by a Mr. I.E. Matthes of the United States Geological Survey, stating, "that somewhere in this immediate vicinity the meteors came to earth – whether on land or sea is a matter of conjecture." *Hyannis Patriot*, September 24, 1923.

Waterspout, from *Nimrod of the Sea* by William M. Davis.

CHAPTER 9
Some Local Folk

Cape Cod's most prolific author, Joseph Crosby Lincoln, found a gold-mine of local characters as subjects for his early twentieth century novels. The Cape is notorious for producing many examples of eccentrics and quirky geniuses. From the sea captain who kept Siamese twins in his barn, to dancing masters and movie stars. And from a Sandwich attorney who reportedly never charged a client more than $9.99, to a summer resident who invented a dog biscuit, unconventional individuals have been a regular and recurring part of our history. Lest you worry, you can be assured that the supply of these characters is far from exhausted.

■ ■ ■

Stephen Hopkins, one of the original Pilgrims, was the first man to build a house in Yarmouth. In 1638, he was granted the right "to erect a house at Mattacheese, and cut hay to winter his cattle, provided it be not to withdraw him from the town of Plymouth." Hopkins, who had earlier attempted to settle in Jamestown, Virginia, didn't stay in Yarmouth long. He turned his house over to his son Giles the same year. Stephen Hopkins is credited with another "first." He reportedly was the first person in Plymouth Colony to own a horse. *Saints and Strangers*, by George F. Willison, page 314.

■ ■ ■

In his journal, William Bradford kept copious notes concerning the Pilgrim families and their plight – of both saints and strangers, alike. His journal also documented those who came in the two subsequent ships that arrived after the *Mayflower* – those ships being the *Fortune* and the *Anne*. According to Bradford, writing in 1650, thirty years after their arrival, "Of these 100. persons which came over in this first ship together, the greater halfe dyed in the generall mortality; and the most of them in 2. or three months time ... of the old stock ... there are yet living this present year, 1650. nere 30. persons." *Of Plimoth Plantation*, by William Bradford.

■ ■ ■

Well after Bradford's own death (in 1657), someone provided an update to the Governor's journal, as written in a different hand is the following commentary: "Twelfe persons liveing of the old stock this present yeare, 1679." The record continued some years later with this: "Two persons liveing that came over in the first shipe 1620, this present yeare, 1690. Resolved White and Mary Chusman (Cushman), the daughter of Mr. Allerton." And finally this note: "Mary Cushman is still living, this present year, 1698."

Mary Cushman was born Mary Allerton around 1616, making her quite young during the *Mayflower* voyage which she made with her father, Isaac, and her mother, Mary, and her two siblings, Bartholomew and Remember. Mary later married Thomas Cushman, who arrived at Plymouth in 1621 aboard the *Fortune*. Cushman was a teenager when he arrived and was left in Bradford's care as the boy's father, Robert, headed back to England on business, where he later died. As a result of the father's death, Bradford adopted Cushman.

Thomas and Mary were married in either 1635 or 36, and "hath 4. children" in 1650 according to Bradford. Thomas died in 1691, in his eighties, while Mary Cushman passed in 1699, also in her eighties, as the last living *Mayflower* Pilgrim. *Of Plimoth Plantation*, by William Bradford; *Saints and Strangers*, by George F. Willison.

■ ■ ■

The first female teacher in the town of Falmouth was Hannah Sargent. She was appointed in 1716 for a sum of "twelve pounds and diet." She was still working in the same capacity in 1724 with the same salary. Perhaps because of her faithful service, she received the added benefit that year of "the use of a horse twice in the year that she might visit her friends." *History of Barnstable County*, Simeon Deyo, editor, p. 652.

■ ■ ■

Titus Winchester was a slave in Sandwich in the late 18th century. He was the property of Reverend Abraham Williams, pastor of the First Parish Church. Offered his freedom at the time of the Revolution, Winchester refused, preferring to stay with his master. He was

68

38 years old when Reverend Williams' death set him free. He went to sea and made his fortune, eventually returning to Sandwich in 1806.

In his will, Winchester stipulated that whatever was left in his estate should go toward purchasing a two-faced clock for the church. In 1808, when he died, his wishes were carried out and the clock was installed in a new steeple. Both clock faces were painted black in honor of the patron who had donated them.

The clock ran well for 65 years until one night in 1873 something went wrong with the mechanism and the device chimed over 400 times before going silent forever. Interestingly, the building, no longer a church, still has a bell tower with a four-sided clock. The individual faces of the clock are painted black. Titus Winchester has not been forgotten. *"Two Hundred and Fiftieth Anniversary Celebration of Sandwich and Bourne at Sandwich, Massachusetts,"* by Ambrose E. Pratt, September 3, 1889.

■ ■ ■

Lucy Lombard, born in Barnstable in 1776, married Josiah Hamblen and moved with him to Montpelier, Vermont. When her husband died in 1803, she rode horseback with her infant daughter, Polly, the several hundred miles back to Hyannis where she later married her late husband's brother, Zacchaeus. *Barnstable Patriot*, February 25, 1954.

■ ■ ■

Captain Ebenezer Weeks, a nineteenth century mariner from Harwich, learned discipline early in life. As a boy, he and his father made a seven-mile walk to the North Parish meeting house to attend Sunday services. Halfway there, the two stopped to rest and have a drink of water at a friend's house. Ebenezer studied the wooden water dipper and decided he could make a similar one that could be used by his family. The next day, he turned out a nice copy of the dipper and took it to his father. At first, Ebenezer's father was pleased with the work his young son had done. But when told of the object's inspiration the previous day, the father scolded the boy for entertaining worldly thoughts on the Lord's Day. *Harwich Men of the Sea* by the Harwich Historical Commission, page 35.

■ ■ ■

The fishing schooner *Premium* was a regular visitor to the Grand Bank fishing grounds. The vessel was owned and operated by Native Americans from Mashpee. Her skipper was Captain Israel Amos, a full-blooded Wampanoag. *Barnstable Patriot*, September 20, 1843.

■ ■ ■

Captain Daniel Bacon, a prominent 19th century Barnstable shipmaster, once housed Siamese twins in his woodshed. They had been brought to this country to be exhibited in a circus by Abel Coffin, one of the captain's mates. *Some Merchants and Sea Captains of Old Boston*, published by State Street Trust Company, Boston, Mass., page 32.

■ ■ ■

A Cape Cod Native American once rode in Buffalo Bill's Wild West Show. Eben Queppish, a member of the Mashpee Wampanoag tribe, was working for a promoter named "Montana Charlie" when he was spotted by William Cody, who hired him away from his first boss. Queppish worked for Cody for a season as a bareback rider but apparently didn't like it all that much. Described as "not an enthusiastic horseman," he left the show and returned to his native Mashpee where he spent the rest of his life as a cook and a hunting guide for vacationing sportsmen. *Mashpee: The Story of Cape Cod's Indian Town*, by Francis G. Hutchins, page 137.

■ ■ ■

Before there was Arthur Murray, there was John H. Foster of Sandwich. Born in 1853, Foster traveled to Europe as a young man and stayed to build a very successful chain of dancing studios in several of the major capital cities of the continent. At one time he taught social dancing to England's King George V and Queen Mary. He eventually came back to his hometown and built a mansion overlooking Cape Cod Bay in the Spring Hill section of East Sandwich, which he called "Masthead." An unusual feature of the house was a game room that was designed to look like the stern section of a Spanish galleon. *A Sandwich Album*, by Rosanna and John Nye Cullity.

■ ■ ■

Robert Ripley's "Believe It or Not" once featured a cartoon about attorney Seth Freeman Nye of Sandwich [1791-1856]. "Seth Nye, an attorney of Sandwich, Mass., for years before his death in 1856 never charged any client more than $9.99 because he felt no lawyer could justify a fee of $10.00." From Sandwich archives – Seth Nye folder.

■ ■ ■

In January of 1877, Augusta Rich made a tour of her hometown village of Osterville and wrote down a few comments about things as she saw them. Her reminiscences were later published in the *Barnstable Patriot*. Augusta probably didn't make everyone happy with her observations. Of Cordelia Crosby, she wrote: "You will remember Mr. Asa Crosby, our village storekeeper. He married Cordelia Bassett of Hyannis. Well, Mr. Crosby died and Cordelia, very curiously, welcomed a tin peddler into her snug home. She meant life good. I think she sold her home rights for a mess of eels. We are all liable to mistakes, but often realize it only when it's too late to amend."

■ ■ ■

The *Yarmouth Register* carried an interesting story on January 1, 1881. "Mr. Albert M. Robbins of Harwich, who left that place last October, ostensibly to visit his sister at Buzzards Bay station, but did not go there, has been heard from for the first time this week, a letter having been received from him from Liverpool England. He was doubtless laboring under some sort of mental difficulty."

■ ■ ■

Lester Coville and Wilton Linnell grew up in Cummaquid in the late 1800's. They were close friends. In 1894, at the age of eleven, Wilton moved with his family to Cotuit. It wasn't until 60 years later that they spoke to each other again. In May of 1955, Wilton made his first visit back to Cummaquid since leaving that village more than a half century earlier. He inquired about his boyhood chum and found that Lester was running a butcher shop in the village. Now in their early 70's, the two met and reminisced about the old days and they had their picture taken together. Later in the day, Wilton got into his car and returned to Cotuit, a distance of less than twenty miles. They never spoke to each other again. *Barnstable Patriot*, May 1955.

■ ■ ■

Under the category of "perseverance" comes the story of the A.B. Nye & Company paint shop in downtown Hyannis. Three times over a twelve-year period, from the Boston Store/Cash Building fire of March 1892 to the great Main Street fire of 1904, Mr. Nye's paint shop was destroyed. As printed in the December 5, 1904 issue of the *Barnstable Patriot*, "A. B. Nye's paint shop was burned out for the third time ... In the rear of the Eagleston building was A.B. Nye & Co.'s paint shop. Here about all the stock that could be handled was removed. As above stated this was Mr. Nye's third fire and he profited by previous experience and commenced work early."

According to the March 8, 1892 issue of the *Patriot*, Mr. Nye was at home sick when the first fire started on a Friday morning. "He occupied the upper floor of the Cash building and besides his own stock and materials had a half dozen carriages which he was painting or varnishing, and a new grocery wagon just built ... Mr. Nye's individual loss is about $1500 to $1600. He had $600 insurance." In between these two large fires was a smaller fire early on a Sunday morning in March 1894 that saw Mr. Nye's paint shop and Mr. Nelson E. Brown's blacksmith shop destroyed. This fire originated in Nye's shop. A local resident named James Brushingham, "who occupies a little cabin near the railroad freight house," first noticed the blaze. All the contents in Mr. Nye's shop, which was 40 feet by 40 feet, were destroyed. As for the blacksmith shop, although the building was a total loss, all items were saved.

And as for A. B. Nye, he rebuilt and carried on. *Barnstable Patriot*, March 8, 1892 & December 5, 1904; *Hyannis Patriot*, March 27, 1894.

■ ■ ■

In 1905, Provincetown native Albert G. Smith engraved the letters of the alphabet three times on the head of a common pin, breaking the record of two times set by Clarence K. Young of the United States Engraving Bureau. *Yarmouth Register*, July 22, 1905.

■ ■ ■

A summer resident of the village of Hyannis Port, Carleton Ellis patented the familiar bone-shaped dog biscuit in 1911. A prolific inventor, Ellis, who had a winter home in Montclair, New Jersey, in 1927 patented the waxed cap used on milk bottles. *Barnstable Patriot*, February 10, 1938.

■ ■ ■

Miss Lillian Drew of Centerville was the first piano player in the first movie house on Cape Cod. The year was 1914 and Varnum's Motion Pictures were being shown in the Masonic Hall on Main Street in Hyannis. In a 1954 recollection, Miss Drew (Lillian Drew Geer) mentioned that in those silent picture days there was a man by the name of Philip Hughes of Hyannis who attended the pictures. He was a horse lover and whenever he saw a scene of someone abusing a horse, he would shout, "Gosh darn you. If I could get my hands on you, I'd fix you!" Sometimes he would get so agitated that the language was a bit more profane. "He owned horses," recalled Miss Drew. "And he was a kindly fellow who couldn't bear to see man or beast hurt." *Barnstable Patriot*, March 11, 1954.

■ ■ ■

"Cape Cod Charlie," the silent era movie star who was a box of-fice attraction for Fox Studios in the 1920's, was technically not from Cape Cod, but he could see the Cape from his boyhood home. Charles Farrell, who starred in a number of films opposite actress Janet Gaynor, was born in Onset, Massachusetts on August 9, 1901. A handsome and athletic young man, Farrell dropped out of Boston University to take up acting. His first picture, "Old Ironsides," came out in 1926 and his career skyrocketed. When paired with Gaynor, the two became America's romantic screen couple. Farrell later acted in television shows during the 1950's, including "My Little Mar-gie." His greatest claim to fame came outside of the theater when he founded the very successful Hollywood Racquet Club in Palm Springs, California. Farrell was later elected mayor of Palm Springs, a position that he held for seven years (1953-1960). He died in 1990 and is buried in Palm Springs. www.goldensilents.com.

■ ■ ■

Frederick Tudor of Sandwich once held the license plate number "1" in Massachusetts. He secured the number the first year that the state issued automobile registration tags and held the valued single digit for over twenty years until his death. *Cape Cod Magazine*, August 1, 1927, page 16.

■ ■ ■

When Mary Heaton Vorse submitted her manuscript, *Time and the Town: A Provincetown Chronicle*, to Dial Press in New York, she was hoping that the publisher would come up with an eye-catching cover that would boost sales. When the first edition arrived in stores, Vorse was mortified to see that the cover featured the very recogniz-able Motif #1 from Rockport, Mas-sachusetts. Apparently, the publish-er wasn't able to distinguish Cape Ann from Cape Cod. Subsequent editions of the book eventually corrected the cover.

■ ■ ■

Chief Storekeeper Stanley Baker of South Dennis may have been the oldest enlisted sailor in the history of the U.S. Navy. Baker

first enlisted in March of 1892. In June of 1940, when he had already served 41 years, with a break between 1901 and 1908, the Navy Department notified his commanding officer that Baker "should be retained in your command as long as he desires." He was then 71 years old. *Yarmouth Register*, March 22, 1941.

■ ■ ■

Warren Lincoln of Brewster was a colorful character. After a long career as a sea captain, he left the water and opened a dry goods store across the street from School House Pond. Later in life, as he approached 80, he got religion and he would write different verses of scripture on his grocery bills. "Verily, verily, I say unto you, if a man keep my savings, he shall never see death," was an example. Below each of these verses, he would always add the one from Romans 13:8, "Owe no man anything." *The Cape Codder*, March 21, 1946.

CHAPTER 10
Visitors to Our Sandy Shores

At one time or other, just about everyone puts a foot on Cape Cod. In a few instances, they've left behind their entire body. Red Skelton, Babe Ruth, Marlon Brando, Helena Rubinstein, Van Cliburn, Bill Clinton, and even Bugs Bunny have all left their mark on the Cape. Some stayed for just a short time. Others, like the 19th century stage actor Joe Jefferson, who is buried in Sandwich, chose to spend eternity here.

■ ■ ■

When Gray Gables was the summer White House for President Grover Cleveland, it wasn't uncommon for local people to have informal contact with the chief executive. On one occasion when some men were clearing brush around his property, the president ambled by to see how the job was going. Cleveland greeted Bradford White, who was supervising the workers, and expressed some impatience at the pace of the work.

"Isn't there anything we can do to hurry the job along, Brad?"

"I dunno – maybe so," replied White. "They're doin' pretty well. And I'm busy seein' that they do it right. But if you're in a real hustle, Mr. President, supposin' you peel off your coat and vest. There's a shovel and a dump cart over there."

The president stopped for a moment and then laughed. As he turned toward his house he looked back at White and said, "Let's just leave it supposin'." *Yarmouth Register*, May 10, 1940.

■ ■ ■

Jan Masaryk, who became president of Czechoslovakia in the years after World War II, spent the fall of 1926 in Woods Hole on vacation with his wife. *Cape Cod Magazine*, June 15, 1927.

■ ■ ■

At one point the search for the kidnapped child of Charles Lindbergh centered on Cape Cod. During the first week of April in 1932, a sea plane piloted by Colonel Lindbergh was seen circling the Cape and Islands. The aircraft eventually landed for a brief time at Cuttyhunk Island. This was after a clerk in a Hyannis store turned a dollar bill into authorities that appeared to be one of the marked pieces of currency that had been supplied to the kidnapper. The bill, however, was off by two digits and not a match. *Yarmouth Register*, April 9, 1932.

■ ■ ■

Comedian "Red" Skelton was Master of Ceremonies at the "Mid Cape Gardens," an entertainment spot in Harwich Port, during the 1930's.

■ ■ ■

Gertrude Lawrence, the famous star of the English and American theater, got into the cranberry business during World War II. She and her husband Richard Aldrich purchased a seven-acre bog in East Dennis near their summer house. They joined the Cranberry Canners Association. "I love being a farmer," the actress told a reporter. "I feel a lot of satisfaction knowing that my berries are helping to feed the armed forces and our own civilian population." *Yarmouth Register*, October 16, 1942.

■ ■ ■

Following World War II, in an effort to promote cranberries as a year round product, the National Cranberry Association began a marketing campaign to connect cranberry sauce with chicken. It seemed a logical extension of the Thanksgiving tradition to have the berry become a regular partner with the bird that was actually a far more popular dinner item than was the turkey. In October of 1948, during National Cranberry Week, a "wedding" was held in South Carver which featured a person decked out in a can of Ocean Spray cranberry sauce joining another person wearing a chicken suit in commercial wedlock. Despite all the excitement, and the presence of a young actor by the name of Charlton Heston who crowned the Cranberry King and Queen, the marketing effort didn't get much response from the public. *The Cranberry: Hard Work and Holiday Sauce*, by Stephen Cole and Lindy Gifford, page 147.

■ ■ ■

Bugs Bunny came to Cotuit in the summer of 1962. Well, sort of. July of that year saw the visit of famed Warner Brothers artist/director Chuck Jones, the winner of two Oscars for his work on Looney Tunes shorts, as well as the recipient of an Academy Lifetime Achievement Award. In fact, his classic cartoon, *What's Opera, Doc?* which features Bugs Bunny and Elmer Fudd against the backdrop of Richard Wagner's operatic music, is considered the greatest cartoon of all time and was honored by the National Film Registry as a "culturally, historically, and aesthetically significant film."

Jones was scheduled to appear at the Cotuit Library on Saturday, July 7th while on vacation with his wife. According to a newspaper report, "He started with Warner Brothers 25 years ago as an 'in-betweener,' a beginner cartoonist who draws 'in-between' action of cartoon characters, while (the) chief cartoonist makes main movements, then went on to become a full-fledged animator, then a director of animated cartoons. Bugs Bunny, Porky Pig, and Daffy Duck are the characters he helped to develop ... since Cotuit in the summer furnishes the locale and inspiration for many an artist, Chuck's watercolor and oil paintings demonstrate his talents in those media. He has had two one-man shows with his paintings." *Barnstable Patriot*, June 28, 1962.

■ ■ ■

Those who think summer traffic jams on Cape Cod are only a recent occurrence should know that a half century ago getting from "Point A" to "Point B" might mean a bumper-to-bumper crawl. With throngs of visitors making their annual pilgrimage to the Cape, it seems travelling around Hyannis in 1962 – whether by car, by bicycle, or by foot – was no easy task, as illustrated by the following:

"One of our pressmen told us last week that it took him one hour and 17 minutes to get from Pleasant Street, Hyannis to his home in Dennis Port. Good thing he doesn't try it for lunch ...The wigging and the wagging that goes on with these untried bike riders gives one cause for grave concern. Perhaps a course in bicycle driving should be offered at rental places ... With the number of cars around town, it seems easier all around to walk wherever possible. But have you tried it lately? Wherever there are sidewalks one is often forced to walk in the street because property owners have neglected to trim their shrubs and they have grown right over the path. And have you noticed the travel trash along the gutters and sidewalks?" *Barnstable Patriot*, July 19, 1962.

■ ■ ■

Van Cliburn, celebrated pianist, played the inaugural concert for the new Cape Cod Conservatory Center when it opened in August of 1973.

■ ■ ■

Bill Clinton might never have been president if, on a visit to Cape Cod in 1966 while a student at Georgetown University, he hadn't been saved from drowning by his friend Fife Symington – a man who later became Governor of Arizona. "I nearly drowned after failing to hold on to a barnacle covered rock in an effort that shredded my hands, arms, chest, and legs," recalled the 42nd president. He never said where this incident occurred, but then, the 42nd president was often vague on many details about his life. "*My Life*," by Bill Clinton, page 72.

■ ■ ■

Not all visitors to the area were of the species *Homo sapiens*. Wolves arriving from off-Cape were such a menace to local livestock in the early 18th century that residents of the peninsula discussed the building of a fence, which "would have been a little N. and W. of the projected canal intended to unite 'Barnstable and Manomet Bays,'" according to Nathanial Freeman's *History of Cape Cod*, Volume 1. In the days before the canal, the fence would have run from Cape Cod Bay to Buzzards Bay, "between Sandwich and Plymouth, to Wayquauset Bay in Wareham," essentially cutting off Cape Cod from the mainland. Although the town of Sandwich was in favor of building such a fence, Falmouth was against it, as were some towns "beyond the county limits ... as they did not wish all the wolves to be shut out of the county upon their own limits." As a result, the fence was never built.

■ ■ ■

In 1912, an antlered visitor arrived on Martha's Vineyard, becoming the first of its kind on the island in half a century. "A sleek and stately buck deer with an impressive set of antlers, is a startling summer visitor to Martha's Vineyard," reported an August 5, 1912 *Barnstable Patriot* article. "He is the first of his tribe to succeed in swimming across Vineyard Sound from Naushon Island," an astonishing feat as the article reminded its readers that Naushon is some four miles away. "For 50 years no deer has stood on Martha's Vineyard island until this buck's arrival."

CHAPTER 11
War Stories

From the Colonial wars of the seventeenth century to the conflicts of our own age, wars have produced interesting consequences for Cape Codders. Whole sections of towns migrated to other places following particular campaigns. Land grants, pensions, and local heroes were the products of conflicts now long forgotten.

■ ■ ■

Gorham, Maine has a direct connection with Cape Cod. In 1727, the Massachusetts Legislature granted land in the province to families of veterans of King Philip's War.

The new settlement was named after Captain John Gorham of Yarmouth, who had been one of the military leaders in the campaign against the Native Americans in 1675. The first settler of the new town was Captain John Phinney of Barnstable, who moved there in 1736, followed by a number of other Cape Cod families. There is a monument in the center of the town for the town's actual founder, Captain John Phinney of Cape Cod. *Cape Cod*, by Charles Swift, page 158.

■ ■ ■

Many people believe the anger over "No taxation without representation," did not surface until patriots like James Otis began to speak out in the 1760's. In fact the issue of fair representation for the colonies arose much earlier, in the late 17th century. In 1686, under the new British government of King James II, Parliament attempted to centralize royal authority in New England by abolishing the individual colonies and substituting a Dominion government headed by a royal governor. Sir Edmond Andros was sent to Boston to administer the new arrangement.

Almost immediately, Andros instituted a number of taxes and regulations without the consent of elected representatives. For towns on the Cape, the regulation that all drift whales that came ashore should be the property of the crown was particularly grievous. Towns had always used the revenue that came from stranded whales to support their ministers, schools, and otherwise pad out their budgets. Under the Dominion system, town meetings were limited, the currency was devalued, and real estate taxes increased—all without benefit of representation.

Believing their rights as Englishmen to be in jeopardy, Cape Codders, along with other New Englanders, were at the point of rebellion. Only the fall of King James II in the Glorious Revolution in 1689 took the pressure off. That same year, royal governor Andros was sent back to England as a prisoner and colonial life resumed its normal pattern. And the cry of "No taxation without representation," was put to sleep for almost another 80 years.

■ ■ ■

"Silver John Goodspeed" of Barnstable got his colorful name while serving aboard a privateer during the French and Indian Wars. Following the capture of a Spanish ship which was carrying a load of silver dollars and silver bars, the vessel was brought into Boston where she was condemned for forfeit. As a means of dividing up the prize, the captain of the privateer made a deal with his crew. Each sailor could have as much silver as he could transport from the end of Long Wharf, where the ship lay, to the head of King Street on the condition that if he stopped to rest along the way—even for a minute, he would lose it all. Goodspeed, as ship's carpenter, was entitled to only a small amount of the prize, but he was quick to realize that the captain had not specified *how* the coins must be carried. The clever carpenter used the ship's boat and loaded coins aboard it. He then rowed non-stop to shore where he was able to claim more than five thousand dollars in silver. *Genealogical Notes of Barnstable Families*, by Amos Otis, 1979 edition page 402.

■ ■ ■

There were four Cape Cod men who participated in the Boston Tea Party. They were Edmund Sears of Brewster, Elisha Mathews of Yarmouth, Joseph Bassett, also of Yarmouth, and Ephraim Smith of Truro. There was also a fifth Cape Codder present at the event on December 16, 1773 and that was Reuben Hall of Dennis, who was a

JACK SHEEDY PHOTO

Orleans Civil War monument.

crewmember aboard one of the Nantucket based tea ships. Information from George Quintal Jr., an official with the Boston Tea Party exhibit.

■ ■ ■

After the September 1774 march of the "Body of the People" prevented the royal Court of Common Pleas in Barnstable from sitting, the building never again served as a King's court. A little over a year later, in the fall of 1775, the court reconvened with newly appointed judges, under the authority of "the government and people of Massachusetts

81

Bay." As a final symbol of rebellion against the crown, and before the session was called to order, the royal coat of arms, which had been required to "be set up in every court of justice," was summarily taken out of the building and burned by the common hangman. *Sketch of the Third Baptist Church and Meeting House with Membership Enrollment*, by Lizzie S. (Hinckley) Crocker, published in 1927, page 19.

■ ■ ■

"A long awaited Pension." After being widowed for sixty years, Molly Downs of Yarmouth was finally granted a pension in 1837 by the U.S. Government for her husband's service in the Revolutionary War. Molly and Benjamin Downs married in 1777. Just a month after the wedding, Benjamin volunteered for service and shortly thereafter died. Molly lived as a wife for 30 days and as a widow for 60 years before the government finally got around to placing on its pension list the name of Benjamin's widow, a woman over 80 years old – Molly Downs of Yarmouth. From the *Niles Weekly Register* and *Boston Transcript*, April 15, 1837: Dennis Historical Society records.

■ ■ ■

During the War of 1812, British ships regularly called at Provincetown, Truro, and Wellfleet. The blockading ships entered into agreements with farmers in these lower Cape Cod towns to supply the fleet with stores, which were paid for in gold at the market price. In the early months of the war, relations between the two parties were so cordial that the chaplain of the British warship *Guerriere*, a Mason, was invited into Provincetown by members of the King Hiram's lodge to address the members of the Cape tip Masonic order. *Every First Monday: A History of King Hiram's Lodge, Provincetown and Its Members*, by James Theriault.

■ ■ ■

In the early days of the Civil War, Eliphalet Doane of Marstons Mills attempted to enlist in the Union army. He was turned down because he was already in his mid-30's and had lost most of his teeth. Doane was, however, a persistent man and was able to convince the town to pay for a new set of teeth so he could fight for his country. Serving in some of the worst battles of the war as a member of the 58th Division of Massachusetts Volunteers, Doane met his end at Petersburg, Virginia on July 20, 1864 when he was shot in the abdomen and died. He left a widow and four children. *Barnstable: Three Centuries of a Cape Cod Town*, by Donald G. Trayser, page 152.

■ ■ ■

During the Civil War, Captain Frederick Nickerson of Dennis was serving as a U.S. Navy pilot. It was Nickerson's job to bring the *U.S.S. Monitor* to Norfolk, Virginia where the ironclad vessel eventually engaged the *C.S.S. Merrimack* at Hampton Roads. While aboard, Captain Nickerson met the Captain of the *Monitor*, whose name was John L. Worden. It turned out that the man was a direct descendent of Peter Worden, the first English settler to live in East Dennis way back in 1639. *Dennis: From First Comers to New Comers*, by Nancy Thacher Reid, page 413.

■ ■ ■

Back in September of 1904, the south coast of Martha's Vineyard must have been quite a noisy place, and few islanders probably got a decent night's sleep, as this brief mention in the local newspaper will attest: "The battleships of the North Atlantic fleet are engaged in target practice, on the range off the south shore of Martha's Vineyard Island, where they and other vessels will be firing at night as well as day during the greater part of the month. The reports of the heavy guns are plainly heard in this section." *Barnstable Patriot*, September 12, 1904.

■ ■ ■

A plane crash at West Dennis in 1932 resulted in one fatality that had connections reaching back to the trenches of World War I, and even as far as the continent of Australia. On board the aircraft was a 36-year-old WWI veteran named Thomas Skeyhill, an Aussie regimental signaler with the 8th Battalion, 2nd Victorian Infantry Division, who had been blinded in 1915 at Cape Helles. He went on to write poetry about the war, published in the book *Soldier Songs From Anzac*, earning him the title "The Blind Soldier Poet." One such poem in the collection, entitled "My Little Wet Home in the Trench," presented a grim picture of the common foot soldier's plight:

> *"I've a little wet home in the trench,*
> *Which the rain-storms continually drench,*
> *Blue sky overhead,*
> *Mud and clay for a bed,*
> *And a stone that we use for a bench."*

Skeyhill toured throughout the world, reciting his poetry and helping to raise money for the Red Cross. During his 1917 visit to

North America he befriended Theodore Roosevelt. The former president put Skeyhill in touch with his personal physician, who eventually restored his eyesight. Skeyhill went on to write a biography about Sergeant Alvin York, which was filmed a number of years later starring Gary Cooper in the title role.

By 1932, Skeyhill and his wife had a summer home in West Dennis. On the day of the accident, his brother-in-law was at the controls of the plane as he tried to land at Skeyhill's home when the aircraft struck some wires and plummeted to the ground. Skeyhill suffered a broken thigh, and died the next day of a pulmonary embolism. He was buried at West Dennis with full military honors. *Yarmouth Register*, May 27, 1932; *Soldier Songs From Anzac*, by Thomas Skeyhill; rpo.library.utoronto.ca; www.adb.online.anu.edu.au.

■ ■ ■

At the beginning of World War II, the U.S. government leased a number of coastal areas along the southern shoreline of Cape Cod. The beaches were set aside for the amphibious landing training that would later bring victory in both the European and Pacific theaters of war. In July of 1942, "Camp Candoit" was established on the shores of Cotuit Bay. In July of 1944, its training mission completed, the same camp was renamed Camp "Havdonit." *Down Ramp: The Story of the Army Amphibian Engineers*, by Brigadier General William Heavey, page 9.

■ ■ ■

During World War II, John F. Kennedy was aboard the *USS Rochambeau* headed out to the Pacific to his PT boat duty station in the New Hebrides. At some point in the voyage, he learned that a Brewster man, Samuel Hall Whitley, was one of the ship's navigators. Kennedy had never formally met the Cape Codder, but during a wardroom conversation he learned that Whitley had been a competitive sailor before the war and had sailed against the future president in yacht regattas in Hyannis Harbor. *The Kennedys at War: 1937-1945*, by Edward Renehan Jr., page 237.

CHAPTER 12
Magnificent Men and Women in Their Flying Machines

The early part of the 20th century was a fabulous time in the arena of manned flight. With the Wright Brothers' success at Kitty Hawk came a barrage of attempts to push back the envelope of the wild blue yonder. Cape Cod saw the arrival of aircrafts and airships, and even a brief encounter with Germany's Graf Zeppelin.

■ ■ ■

One such attempt to push back the blue envelope had a brush with Cape Cod and the Islands in 1910 when journalist-turned-adventurer Walter Wellman attempted to become the first person to cross the Atlantic Ocean in an airship.

Wellman had earlier attempted, and failed three times, to reach the North Pole via airship. He next turned his attention to transatlantic flight, which culminated in an attempt in October 1910 as reported in the *Sandwich Observer* newspaper: "Walter Wellman and five others left Atlantic City Saturday morning (October 15) at about 8 o'clock in the big airship *America* to cross the Atlantic." According to the newspaper report, "The *America* passed Nantucket at 10:30 a.m. Sunday."

But the airship would only get as far as 140 miles northeast of the island before being blown off course. The dirigible developed engine trouble and eventually ditched on October 18 about 360 miles off Cape Hatteras where Wellman and his crew, and apparently a cat that was onboard, were rescued by the *RMS Trent* under the command of a Captain Downs. Despite the failed transatlantic attempt, the flight briefly set a record for the longest such flight for an airship. *Sandwich Observer*, October 18 & 25, 1910, January 3, 1911.

■ ■ ■

Aircraft and airships first arrived on Cape Cod in the nineteen-teens, notably in connection with the annual agricultural fair as illustrated by the following: "Phillips Ward Page of the Burgess & Curtis Co., who will operate the airships at the Fair Tuesday and Thursday, says that flying as a sport really arrived with the perfection of the hydro-aeroplane ... There will be a parachute drop from the hydroplane into the water, carrier pigeons let loose from the aeroplane in the air to fly back to Marblehead; day light fire-works from the aeroplane." *Barnstable Patriot*, August 26, 1912.

■ ■ ■

The sighting of an airship slipping the tethers of earth was cause for some excitement here on the Cape, and in the pages of the local newspaper. For instance, "Summer residents at the head of Buzzards Bay saw an airship cruising in the vicinity Tuesday. The air craft was seen to fly over Plymouth, across to Woods Hole, over to Wings Neck, and then back in the direction of Woods Hole." *Barnstable Patriot*, August 5, 1912.

■ ■ ■

And this from the July 15, 1918 issue of the *Hyannis Patriot*: "Hyannis Park was treated to a grand display of airship manoeuvres last week which were very interesting to a large number of people. The airship landed in the bay five times. We hope to see them often." But it was not all fun and games. In 1916, Nantucket was "to be connected with the mainland by telephone for the first time during this coming summer ... The island's isolation is to be further broken next summer by delivery of mail in airships." *Barnstable Patriot*, March 6, 1916.

■ ■ ■

What better way to make a fashionable arrival on the Cape during the roaring 1920's than via airship as documented by the following: "Two airships made landing at Pilgrim Heights, North Truro, Saturday, and their occupants were week-end guests of the Sayre family ... We understand Mr. Sayre is in business connected with aircraft and talks of making an airship landing near his home." *Hyannis Patriot*, October 28, 1926.

COURTESY OF THE NICKERSON ROOM, CAPE COD COMMUNITY COLLEGE
Chatham Naval Air Station during World War I.

■ ■ ■

The year 1929 saw impressive airships hovering over Cape Cod landmarks. In September, the appropriately named New England airship *Mayflower* was being used by the Massachusetts Institute of Technology "in connection with the institute's radio research program ... radio experimental flights are being made almost daily over Buzzards Bay," reported the September 12, 1929 issue of the *Hyannis Patriot*. "The ship is one of six built and owned by the Goodyear concern, and is 128 feet in length, with a capacity of 86,000 cubic feet of helium, the non-flammable, non-explosive lifting gas on which America has a monopoly."

■ ■ ■

The headline "Zep Passes the Cape" announced to readers that the German airship *Graf Zeppelin* was seen by a number of Cape Codders as it made its way from Lakehurst, NJ, passing the Cape on its transatlantic voyage back to Germany as part of an around-the-world voyage. The dirigible passed over Nantucket Sound early on a Monday morning. "Mr. and Mrs. Winslow Thacher went out on Great Island in Lewis Bay and saw the air liner as she hove into view

87

from the direction of Woods Hole, and watched it until well over Chatham, when the Zeppelin turned and headed northeast for the long journey across the Atlantic." While the early morning commotion caused by the "giant dirigible" awakened Nelson Bradford "by the vibration of his house as the aircraft passed by over the Bishops." *Barnstable Patriot*, November 1, 1928.

Meanwhile, along the lower Cape, the mammoth German dirigible did not escape the watchful eye of those along the peninsula's elbow: "The *Graf Zeppelin*, on her start for Germany Monday morning was sighted over Chatham at 6:15 am taking an eastward course out to sea." *Harwich Independent*, October 31, 1928.

■ ■ ■

One of the earliest women from Cape Cod to fly an airplane was Ann Smalley of Harwich Port. Right after graduating from Harwich High School in the late 1920's, Ms. Smalley started taking lessons and received her pilot's license before she was 20 years old. She flew in an open cockpit "Jenny" two-seater and was a frequent flying companion with internationally known aviators Ralph Boardman and Frank Crowley. During her flying days, which lasted over 20 years, Ann Smalley was familiar with airports in Falmouth, Marstons Mills, Hyannis, and Eastham. When World War II came, she joined the Coast Guard, graduating as one of the first women officers in a class of men at New London, Connecticut. From a Tales of Cape Cod interview, September 6, 1977.

■ ■ ■

Another woman pilot with Cape connections was Joanna Lillie Fay. Her great-grandfather was Joseph Story Fay, who became a summer resident of Falmouth in the 1850's. Born in 1908, Joanna spent summers in Falmouth and became interested in flying as a teenager. She soloed at the Marstons Mills airport in 1928, at age 20, and received the first private pilot's license given to a woman in Massachusetts. By then she had shortened her name to Joan. A frequent participant in air races around the country in the 1930's, she ended up with over 2,000 hours of flight time by the start of WWII. Moving west, she continued flying in Arizona and is a member of the Arizona Aviation Hall of Fame. From the Fay Family Genealogy Page, www.ancestry.com.

■ ■ ■

At the time when the Hyannis Airport was coming into being, one of its directors was the famous female aviator Amelia Earhart, as mentioned in a number of articles from the *Hyannis Patriot* newspaper in 1928. "There has been much agitation on the Cape of late for a real airport to provide for the needs of the present and future aeronautics ... At last, a group of well-known men, among whom are included several who always have the welfare of Cape Cod at heart, have organized the Hyannis Air-port Corporation. Among those reported as interested ... Miss Amelia Earhart of Boston, the well-known woman pilot who has, until recently held the woman's altitude record..." *Hyannis Patriot*, February 2, 1928.

A June 7, 1928 issue of the *Hyannis Patriot* stated, "Amelia Earhart who is in the public eye today as trans-Atlantic flyer, is interested in the Hyannis Airport" as both "a stockholder and also as a director." While the June 21 issue of the paper announced the upcoming grand opening of the airport, and mentioned that "many prominent people are stockholders ... among them being Miss Amelia Earhart, a director of the Hyannis Airport, who flew across the Atlantic this week and was the first woman to successfully make the hazardous hop."

Additionally, the *Harwich Independent*, in its June 27 issue, made mention of Earhart's flight, referring to her as the "acclaimed queen of the air, or the 'Lady Lindy'" although she "asserts that she was in reality only a passenger on the momentous voyage, although she is an experienced aviator."

The grand opening of the airport was celebrated on September 7, 8, and 9 with "an air meet of gigantic proportions" to feature some "40 or more airships participating in the air races, bombing contests, parachute jumping, and other events" according to the *Hyannis Patriot* of August 2, 1928. "Miss Amelia Earhart of Boston, the only woman flyer to cross the Atlantic in an airplane, and a director of the Hyannis airport, is expected to lend her presence to the scene and take an active part in the air program." While the September 12 issue of the *Harwich Independent* reported, "The opening days of the Hyannis airport drew an immense crowd from all parts of the Cape ... The demonstrations embodied everything expected in airship possibilities ... The meet was truly wonderful." Unfortunately, the dates of the opening conflicted with Miss Earhart's busy schedule and she did not attend.

■ ■ ■

During the years of JFK's presidency, the Kennedy family's aeronautic happenings made the local paper: "Kennedys continue to make the news, not only in Washington but right here at the airport. They're one of the flyingest families in the country ... Ted Kennedy, the president's brother has been coming and going with Cape & Islands Flight Service, sometimes doing the pilot work himself ...

The *Caroline* (the Kennedy's private plane) landed with Mrs. Ethel Kennedy, wife of Attorney-General Robert Kennedy and several of their children and Mrs. Jean Kennedy Smith with her three children, all bound for their summer homes in Hyannis Port. A day or so later Mrs. Rose Kennedy, the president's mother came in on Northeast Airlines from New York just as her daughter-in-law Mrs. Joan Kennedy (Ted's wife) departed on the same aircraft. And more Kennedys are expected to arrive by air this weekend." *Barnstable Patriot*, July 5, 1962.

■ ■ ■

The "Barnstable Municipal Airport" column reported the following during a summer of 1963 entry: "Superb summer weather this past week has sent this terminal into its busy seasonal surge. From every department comes news of stepped-up activity ... The flying Kennedys have launched the summer season with a flurry of air travel. Senator Edward Kennedy chartered C & I for Boston Sunday ... brother-in-law Steve Smith hopped aboard Cape & Islands from Boston Friday and left the same way Monday morning. Mrs. Ethel Kennedy, the wife of the Attorney General, several of the children and a pack of five (maybe four) dogs arrived aboard the family plane *Caroline* ... Arnold Palmer's Aero-Commander dropped in during the U.S. Open proceedings." *Barnstable Patriot*, June 27, 1963.

■ ■ ■

To celebrate their previous day's wedding engagement, Lois Frotten, a 20-year-old Hyannis telephone operator and her fiancé decided to go skydiving out of the Marstons Mills Airport. It was a clear summer day in July of 1962. This was the first time Lois had ever tried skydiving and when she exited the plane, one of her feet got tangled in the parachute lines and the chute didn't open properly. Lois fell about 2,500 feet into Mystic Lake. Fortunately, there were some boaters on the lake and they quickly pulled the stunned woman from the water. Taken to Cape Cod Hospital, she was treated for a broken nose and several broken vertebrae and released. Because of her survival, Lois Frotten became something of a celebrity and appeared on the television show "What's My Line?" Her line was "Never Again!!" *Cape Cod Standard Times*, July 19, 1962.

CHAPTER 13
Oddenda: Perpetual Calendars and Amphi-Cars

Cape Codders have always been known for finding ways to do things differently. From revising the calendar, burning forests to make charcoal, and even driving a car on water, local people have always been ready to put a spin on old ideas while at the same time, adding a few new ones.

■ ■ ■

The first recorded government mail delivery on Cape Cod was in 1654 when the governor of Plymouth colony paid a certain John Smith for carrying letters from Plymouth to Nauset. *History of Barnstable County*, by Simeon Deyo.

■ ■ ■

Several Cape Cod towns once produced charcoal. In Dennis, prior to the Civil War, Jonathan Sears operated one of the so-called "funns" that were used to make it. His operation, which consisted of some cone shaped brick-lined structures where the charcoal was gathered after a slow burning process, was located on the hill above East Dennis village near the present Dennis Pines golf course. The wood was allowed to smolder for several days and then the charcoal would be gathered by a wooden basket sieve. Charcoal was used by blacksmiths in iron making, also in gunpowder making, and it was the base for printers ink. It was even advertised for cleaning teeth and purifying the breath!! Interestingly, with all of the pine trees on Cape Cod, they were not generally used in making charcoal. The pitch could explode into flame and ruin the "sweat" of the process. *A Reverence for Wood*, by Eric Sloan, pages 58, 59.

■ ■ ■

The unique, bright quality that characterized early Sandwich glass was due to the use of barytes. Combined with silex, ash, nitre, pig lead, and other ingredients, barytes was added to the molten glass, giving the finished product a beautiful silver tint that was not duplicated anywhere else. *Sandwich Glass*, by Lenore Wheeler Williams, page 14.

■ ■ ■

Stephen Smith was born into a poor Barnstable family in 1805. As a teenager, he apprenticed himself to a Sandwich cabinetmaker. Eventually he moved to Boston and set up his own woodworking shop. In the mid-1830's he invented the roll top desk and also created the first modern file cabinet. The inventions made Smith a wealthy man. By the 1850's his roll top desks could be found in schools, banks, and business offices across the country. At the 1876 Philadelphia Exhibition, Smith's roll top desk took the $1,000 gold medal prize in the category of office furniture. *"Stephen Smith and His Roll Top Desk,"* by Betty Bearse, published in *New England Galaxy*, Fall 1972, page 58.

■ ■ ■

A Chatham-born man, Willard Edwards, invented what he called the "Perpetual Calendar." Edwards developed a calendar that had the dates falling on the same day each year. By making all but March, June, September, and December have 30 days (the four mentioned would have 31 days), Edwards divided the year into four equal quarters. Instead of having Easter falling as it does on the first Sunday after the first full moon and after the first day of spring, it would always fall on April 14th – a Sunday. Perhaps the best thing about Edwards' calendar is that there would never be a Friday the 13th! Proposed in the 1960's, the idea caught some interest, but then seemed to fade away. Today, few remember Edwards or his calendar. *Cape Cod Standard Times*, June 25, 1972.

■ ■ ■

Another prolific Cape Cod inventor was Luther Childs Crowell, who was born in West Dennis. As a young man he was intrigued by the idea of flight. He built gliders and flew them out of the up-

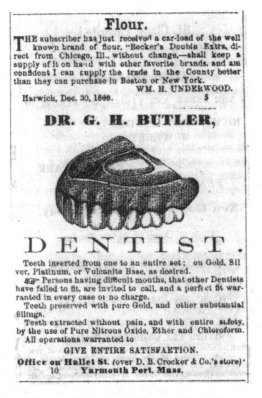

Yarmouth Register, February 25, 1870

stairs loft of a barn near Bass River. In 1862 he received a patent for what he called "a new and improved aerial machine." Nothing much materialized from his interest in aviation and Crowell moved to Boston and got into the printing business. During his time in that business, he patented a large number of inventions to improve and speed up the printing process. He is often given credit for inventing the square-bottomed paper bag, but it would appear that his 1867 patent was for a paper bag-making machine – not one of the square bottom variety. Margaret Knight, a factory worker in Springfield, Massachusetts, seems to have the inside claim to coming up with the idea of the square-bottomed paper bag. Her 1870 patent actually put the square bottom in the paper bags that were being produced with Crowell's earlier invention. In 1873, Crowell was granted patent number 137,533 for a machine that could mass produce the square-bottomed paper bag. *The Cape Cod Voice*, June/July 2005. U.S. Patent office letter August 16, 1872.

■ ■ ■

In January of 1903, Guglielmo Marconi sent the first radio signals across the Atlantic from South Wellfleet. It was a message from President Theodore Roosevelt to Britain's King Edward. When the reply from the King came back, Marconi grabbed local man Charlie Paine to take the just received message to the Wellfleet telegraph office so it could be sent on to Washington. "Drive like the wind," Marconi told Paine. "And if you kill your horse, I'll get you another one!" Paine loved his horse, Diamond, and wasn't going to overtax the animal, even for this momentous achievement. "Well, as soon as I'd driven out of sight, I slowed Diamond down to a walk," Paine later recounted. "We made the depot in good time and the message went out over the wires. Yes, I was pretty excited too, but still I wasn't going to kill my horse – not even for Marconi." *Marconi and His South Wellfleet Wireless*, by John Hinshaw, page 21.

■ ■ ■

In the first years of the 20th century Nantucket banned automobiles. The town bylaw was passed with the approval of the livery stable operators who saw their livelihoods threatened. Mr. Joseph Folger wanted one of the new automobiles in the worst way. In 1910 he purchased a Stanley Steamer and had it shipped to the island. His neighbors warned him that he'd be subject to fines if he took the car out for a spin. But Mr. Folger knew that the state road that went from Nantucket town out to Siasconset at the east end of the island was not under the town's jurisdiction. So when he wanted to use his car, he hitched it up to a horse and team and had it hauled from his barn to the first mile marker of the state road. There he unhitched the car and drove it out and back to Siasconset. When he got back to the first mile marker, he re-hitched the car to his horse and team and hauled it back to his barn. "Ain't no law says you can't use an automobile as a wagon," he told chagrined town officials. In 1917, the bylaw that banned cars was repealed for good. From a Tales of Cape Cod interview with Clara Block, July 26, 1978.

■ ■ ■

It seems in July 1962 a strange beast was sighted in Lewis Bay. That same beast was later seen at Wequaquet Lake, as well as at other bodies of water around Barnstable. No, it wasn't a sea monster, but rather, it was an amphibious automobile – believe it or not!

"Last May our Hyannis correspondent reported the sighting of a disconcerting bit of machinery paddling around Lewis Bay. To quote '... we were a bit taken aback to see an automobile coming towards us in the water…' Well, in the past few weeks it hasn't only been our Hyannis correspondent who has been filled with doubt and wonder. On ponds located all over the town people look up in astonishment while a car cruises by them in the water."

Known as the Amphi-Car, manufactured in West Germany by Karlsruhe Industries, it was registered for use on land and on sea, and was locally owned by Ruth Rusher, a Welfare Department social worker.

"Before entering the water it is necessary to pause to lock the doors … The car is steered through the water by the front wheels. The propeller is engaged by depressing the same clutch pedal as is used on land, operating a gear shift lever to the right of the land shift … If you see it, you can believe it, be it on land or on sea!" *Barnstable Patriot*, July 26, 1962.

COURTESY OF DAVID TUBMAN

Ruth Rusher and her Amphi-Car.

[For the Register.]
First of August in Sandwich.

MR. EDITOR:—

The friends of universal negro emancipation assembled at the Methodist Meeting-house in this village, at 2 o'clock P. M., and listened to an interesting discourse from the Rev. Tho's Ely, on the injustice of Slavery, and the benefits and importance of immediate emancipation—to the country and the world—to the slaveholder and to the slave. The address was closed with an exhortation to united, judicious effort.

The assembly not being large several friends requested its repetition on the next Sabbath, to which the Rev'd gentleman consented.

In the evening two hours were pleasantly and profitably passed away (after prayer) in the discussion of two resolutions, the purport of which was, first, The progress of the reform of civil government, of which the emancipation act of the British Parliament is a bright evidence; and secondly, That the British West India Islands, exhibit an irrefragible proof of the safety, justice and happy results of unconditional freedom to those who are unrighteously enslaved. The speakers were Giles Pease, Tho's Ely, Joseph Mash, J. F. Clarke, Josiah Foster, Samuel H. Allyn.

Although there was not as great a gathering as there was in many other places, in this and other countries on that day, yet there was evidenly no small sympathy manifested for the suffering millions within our own territory. The day was well spent. May it be universally celebrated as a day of rejoicing in all coming time.

JOSEPH MASH.

Sandwich, Aug. 2, 1845.
Will the Patriot please copy?

Notice of an early anti-slavery meeting in Sandwich. From the *Yarmouth Register*, August 7, 1845.

CHAPTER 14
Playing Ball

Cape Codders have always had a penchant for sports. The local Wampanoags participated in a lacrosse-type game called "Baggatiewag," where a skin ball was passed with a crooked stick toward a goal post. From "stoole-ball" played in early Plymouth, and nineteenth century horse racing, to today's huge interest in the Cape Cod Baseball League, games of all kind have been part of the local scene.

■ ■ ■

Ask most folks who invented the game of baseball, and when and where that sport was invented, and you are bound to receive the response: Abner Doubleday, sometime in the mid-19th century, at Cooperstown, New York.

That story has been debated, as it is believed the game of baseball evolved from other similar games brought to the New World by European settlers. For instance, a game somewhat like baseball – called "stoole-ball" – was played here in this country in the early years of the 17th century, just up the road at Plymouth. In fact, the National Baseball Hall of Fame in Cooperstown points to this particular game, played by the Pilgrims in December of 1621, as an early ancestor of the game of baseball we know today.

The game of stoole-ball, or stool ball, dates to medieval times. There were no strict rules, per se, as the game varied slightly from village to village. The general objective was for a pitcher to toss a ball and strike a stool positioned behind a batter; and for the batter to prevent this by hitting the ball with a bat. There was a base located behind the pitcher, toward which the batter would run when he (or she, as the game was played with men and women) hit the ball. If the batter made it back to the stool at home a run would be scored.

On Christmas Day in 1621, a number of Pilgrims, under the direction of Governor William Bradford, were hard at work constructing a fence, as most of the Pilgrims (from the vessels *Mayflower* and *Fortune*, which had arrived at Plymouth earlier that year) did not celebrate Christmas as a Holy Day. Yet, amongst them were some of the non-"Saint" Pilgrims who did wish to honor the holiday, and as such were excused from work detail by Bradford in order that they may make merry. Yet, in the Governor's eyes, the merriment went too far. According to Bradford, these folks were "in ye streete at play, openly; some pitching ye barr, & some at stoole-ball, and shuch like sports."

The ballgame was short-lived, though, as Bradford "tould them that was against his conscience, that they should play & others worke." So he "tooke away their implements," saying that "ther should be no gameing or reveling in ye streets," thus ending the stoole-ball exhibition. Alas, on that December day in 1621 there was no joy in Mudville. From a National Baseball Hall of Fame exhibit; *Of Plimoth Plantation*, by William Bradford; http://slumberland.org/sca; www.pilgrimhall.org.

■ ■ ■

A baseball game was played in Cotuit on a Wednesday afternoon in August of 1896 between the "the home boys – 'Cotuits' and the 'Wianno Beach' team." The contest was described as "one of the best of the season. The home team won the game 9-8, to the joy of the local crowd made up mostly of those from Cotuit and neighboring Osterville who "were pleasingly interested from beginning to the end of game." According to the writer, "Some fine plays were made by both basemen, and fielders of both clubs worthy of more credit than the writer is capable of giving in this short article."

Yet, the one element that the writer did key in on was the trash talk, or rather, lack thereof, which apparently had plagued other games that season. "One thing was very noticeable to the writer, that profanity and cheap talk was left out of the game. That's right boys! Those things never add anything to the game or player." *Hyannis Patriot*, August 19, 1895.

■ ■ ■

If we can allow a bit of fudge in extending Cape Cod's history across Buzzards Bay to Point Independence in Onset, the Cape can claim an unusual sports distinction. The man who invented the "bunt" in baseball spent his last days just a home run distance from Bourne. Dick Pearce was one of the pioneers of the American pas-

COURTESY OF SANDWICH HISTORICAL SOCIETY

Sandwich Baseball Team, 1888 Southeastern Massachusetts Champions.

time. He played for 28 years for various teams during the dawn of professional baseball. He was a shortstop and catcher for the Brooklyn Athletics and played in one of the most memorable games of the 19th century, an 8-7 extra inning victory in 1870 over the Cincinnati Reds, a team that had been unbeaten for 80 games.

But Pearce's most important achievement was in devising a way of getting on base that saw him hitting down on the ball and bouncing it just out in front of home plate. The ball, with the spin he put on it, then bounced into foul territory short of third base. It was impossible to throw Pearce out when he did this. It wasn't until 1876 that the rule was changed to disallow such a hit unless it stayed fair beyond third base. In the meantime, Pearce set all kinds of on base percentage records with his "trick hit." Retiring as an active player in 1883, he did some umpiring for a while before settling down with his wife in Onset. There he stayed until his death in 1908. *Boston Sunday Globe*, December 17, 1905.

■ ■ ■

There is a good chance that the first time a baseball team ever flew to a scheduled game occurred in May of 1919 when the team from the Chatham Naval Air Station boarded several sea planes for the

60-mile over water flight to New Bedford to play an Army team from Fort Rodman. Perhaps it was a bit of airsickness that might explain the Cape team's 12-6 loss at the hands of the Army players. *Wings Over Cape Cod*, by Joseph Buckley, page 99.

■ ■ ■

Babe Ruth on Cape Cod: "George Herman Ruth, better known as 'Babe' visited his close friend Lawrence Nickerson, at the house of Mr. Nickerson's parents, Captain and Mrs. Oscar Nickerson." *Barnstable Patriot*, December 19, 1923.

■ ■ ■

Perhaps the first thought that goes through a person's mind when the name of tennis player Bobby Riggs comes up is the 1970's image of the loud-mouthed, middle-aged chauvinist who bragged that he could beat any woman professional tennis player. Then he had the misfortune to run into Billie Jean King who took him to school and defeated him in the much-ballyhooed "Battle of the Sexes." Few remember that, as a young man, Riggs was actually a pretty good tennis player. In the summer of 1946, Riggs brought his bag of smashes and lob shots to Cape Cod and walked away with the winning trophy in that year's Cape Cod Professional Tennis Tournament. *Cape Cod Standard Times*, July 29, 1946.

■ ■ ■

Chatham was the first town on Cape Cod to construct a building specifically for roller-skating. That was in the year 1882. *Sandwich Observer*, May 22, 1884.

■ ■ ■

The original greens at the Highland Links golf course in North Truro were of rolled gravel. *Truro, Cape Cod, As I Knew It*, by Anthony L. Marshall, page 132.

■ ■ ■

In Harwich, there once was an anti-golf club. It was formed on July 4, 1900. But by the end of July, it had disbanded because the president of the club had learned to play the game. *Barnstable Patriot*, July 31, 1900.

■ ■ ■

Fore!
Cape Cod Magazine, **November 1915**

Casting back to President John F. Kennedy's summer White House years here on Cape Cod, mental images abound of the president and his large family playing touch football games at the Kennedy Compound in Hyannis Port or of JFK sailing in Nantucket Sound aboard his Wianno Senior, *Victura*. Yet, JFK was also an avid golfer, playing at the nearby Hyannis Port Club. According to his press secretary Pierre Salinger, the president shot in the high 70's and low 80's. Salinger indicated that Kennedy had "strong tee shots and deftness around the greens." The former press secretary admitted, though, that JFK's long irons were "erratic." *With Kennedy*, by Pierre Salinger.

101

AFFAIRS ABOUT HOME.

Yarmouth Port and Yarmouth.

BASE BALL.—The first nine of the Matta-keesetts and of the Iyannoughs, played a game on the grounds of the latter, last Friday. The former won, as will be seen by the following summary:

MATTAKEESETT	O.	R.	IYANOUGH.	O.	R.
Davis, c	4	5	Bond, c	2	4
Hallet, p	4	5	Crowell, T. 1b	4	3
Thacher, S. 1b	2	6	Linnell, rf	3	5
Thacher, F. 3b	2	5	Crowell, S. ss	4	3
Phinney, ss	1	8	Eldridge, F. p	2	3
Gorham, W. rf	3	4	Nye, lf	4	3
Sears, 2b	4		dridge, J. 3b	2	6
Bassett, c f			xter, cf	1	5
Gor			well, E. 2b	5	2
				27	34

	NG.	6	7	8	9	
		3	2	4	4—43
		0	0	7	8—34

'5, 1867

— The first nine of the Mattakeesetts, played with the Independents in Sandwich, last Saturday, and the latter won by the following score:

MATTAKEESETT.	O.	R.	INDEPENDENT.	O.	R.
Davis, c	3	4	McMannis, cf	4	4
Hallet, 1b	0	6	Montague, E 3b	5	3
Payne, rf	5	2	Hinkley, 1b	1	5
Thacher, F. 3b	3	4	Fagan, rf	1	6
Phinney, p	1	5	Deene, 2b	4	4
Sears, 2b	1	6	Cannary, ss	5	3
Ryder, cf	3	4	Montague, T p	1	6
Eldredge, ss	4	2	Montague, M c	1	6
Tyler, lf	4	2	Conelley, lf	2	4
	24	35		24	41

RUNS EACH INNING.

	1	2	3	4	5	6	7	8	
Mattakeesett—	6	3	4	4	2	6	5	5	—35
Independent—	4	5	11	4	7	2	3	5	—41

Umpire—J. Montague.

The Yarmouth club was very politely entertained by the Sandwich boys.

Yarmouth Register, November 8, 1867

CHAPTER 15
Flotsam, Jetsam, and Then Some

Lots of strange things drift ashore on the Cape. Some are gone with the next tide. Others stay and become part of the permanent landscape. Here are some items, none of which fit into a particular category, that show the variety of little known and unusual facts and happenings that make Cape Cod such a unique place.

■ ■ ■

There are many conjectures as to whether the Vikings visited Cape Cod. At Aptucxet Trading Post in Bourne there is a reputed rune stone carrying symbols that appear to be of Viking origin. Olaf Strandwold, in his book, *Norse Inscriptions on American Stones*, claims that when translated, the Bourne stone says: "Jesus amply provides for us here and in heaven." Proving that academics don't always agree, another scholar, Harvard University linguist Dr. Barry Fell, claims that the symbols translate to "Proclamation of annexation. Do not deface. Hanno takes possession of this place."

■ ■ ■

There are at least four connections to Paul Revere on Cape Cod. In 1796, King Hiram's Lodge AF & AM in Provincetown had their charter signed by Revere who was then the Masonic Grand Master of Massachusetts. Shortly afterwards, the lodge commissioned Revere to make a twelve-piece set of silver jeweled office medallions. These are still in the possession of the lodge.

A second connection with the Boston silversmith is the 807-pound bell that hangs in the First Congregational Church in Falmouth. It was ordered from Revere's casting shop and installed in the newly built church in 1796. The cost was $338.94. On the outside of the bell is the inscription: "The living to the church I call, and to the grave I summon all." The First Parish Church in Sandwich also received a Revere bell in 1813.

Still another Revere presence can be found in the West Parish Meeting House in West Barnstable. The church has a Revere bell cast in 1806 as a bequest from the Otis family. *Every First Monday: A History of King Hiram's Lodge, Provincetown and its Members*, by James Theriault; *"Falmouth's Revere Bell,"* by Janet Hull, published in *Summerscape 2008*, page 10; *Churches of Cape Cod*, by Marion Vuilleumier, page 18.

■ ■ ■

Mashpee is the only town on Cape Cod never to have been served by a railroad line. *Cape Cod Railroads*, by Robert Farson, page 320 – map of the New York, New Haven, and Hartford railroad system in 1910.

■ ■ ■

Anyone thinking that Cape Cod was an enlightened place on the subject of race in the years prior to the Civil War should take a look at the March 1826 Yarmouth town meeting records. Voters approved an article that year that stipulated that non-whites would be buried in a separate corner of the ancient cemetery in Yarmouth Port. Citizens of mixed blood were given a month's deadline to dig up the remains of their ancestors and move them to the southeast corner of the burying ground. From Yarmouth town meeting records, March 6, 1826.

■ ■ ■

Later in the Cape's history, racism was on display in the June 17, 1905 edition of the *Yarmouth Register*. Under the heading "Color Line in Harwich," there is a report of a special town meeting where whites demanded that children of color be educated in separate schools. "There are a great many natives of the Cape Verde Islands living in the town and those who favor separate schools have argued that the interests of both the white and the Negroes will be served better if the children of each race be separated."

■ ■ ■

The October 22, 1898 edition of the *Yarmouth Register* carried a note that "a band of gypsies are camped out on the Barnstable Road near John Hartnett's farm."

South Orleans.

A GOLDEN WEDDING.—Mr. Freeman H. and Margery A. Rogers, celebrated their fiftieth marriage anniversary the 10th inst., by receiving their children and grand-children, consisting of thirty-six, at the old homestead in So. Orleans.

After a sumptuous repast, presents were collected and presented. Appropriate singing by Celia M. Linnell, was then listened to, followed by a recitation by R. Ella Rogers. It was an occasion of pleasure to all.

Sandwich.

Messrs. H. T. & I. N. Keiths' Car Manufactory commenced operations again on Monday last, working on an order from the Fitchburg R. R. Co., for twenty-five of their patent dump cars.

—Considerable dissatisfaction is manifested in the west and north part of the town, at the prospect of being cut off from the rest of the world by the proposed canal with no means of communication for teams short of Monument. Efforts have been made by petitions and other means that an amendment may be made to the proposed charter, so that a bridge or ferry may be established at West and North Sandwich, public convenience seeming to demand it.

—The Star of Hope Lodge, I. O. of G. T., gave an exhibition in the Town Hall, on Thursday and Saturday evenings, consisting of dialogues, declamations, singing, &c., to very good audiences. Though some of the parts were somewhat overdone, the entertainment was of a high order of excellence. The play of the evening was entitled "Fruits of the wine cup," the characters of which were generally well sustained. The singing by the Lodge, assisted by some fine solos by Mrs. Severance, formerly of West Sandwich, was very good.

■ ■ ■

An old Cape Cod superstition said that to kill a toad would bring on a shower of rain. *Witchcraft in Old and New England*, by George Lyman Kittredge, page 183.

■ ■ ■

At one time it was a custom to place a coin either in the foundation or in one of the sills in new homes that were built on Cape Cod.

■ ■ ■

In the present age, the word "earmark" has negative political connotations. But in the early history of Cape Cod, the use of earmarks was important in distinguishing ownership of cattle that were turned out to graze on the common lands. Truro town records reveal some examples of them.

"The mark of the cattle of Daniel Smalley Jr. of Cape Codd is a slit in the top of the right ear and a nick in each side of the same ear." Recorded by John Snow, Town Clerk, on June 8, 1724.

"Isaac Hopkins hath taken up his deceased father's mark which is a crop of the top of ye right ear and a half crop on ye underside of the left ear." Recorded by Moses Paine, Town Clerk, on March 6, 1753.

■ ■ ■

Another word that has lost meaning over time is the word 'drummer." In the late 19th and early 20th century, peddlers were referred to as drummers. These itinerant merchants would come to the Cape on the train and visit a village, taking orders for merchandise that would later be shipped by railway express. They were, in a sense, and for that time, walking Sears Roebuck catalogs.

■ ■ ■

The old Hotel Nobscussett on the north side of Dennis was originally built as a resort in Scituate, Massachusetts and was known as the Bay House. In 1872, it was disassembled and brought across Cape Cod Bay and set up in the former whaling grounds to the west of Corporation Road. Its first season was in the summer of 1873. The building was renamed the Nobscussett House in 1885 when the property was purchased that year by Charles Tobey. The ornate building with its wide porches was torn down in the spring of 1936, a victim of the Great Depression. *Barnstable Patriot*, November 7, 1935.

■ ■ ■

The Beebe family of Falmouth was known for its eccentricities. Between 1891 and 1898, visitors who were invited for dinner at Tanglewood, one of the family summer homes, were weighed and had their poundage recorded before they were seated in the dining room. Gardner Hammond was the heaviest dinner guest, weighing in at 240 pounds on September 27, 1896. *Falmouth Enterprise*, September 15, 1939.

■ ■ ■

The Sandwich boardwalk, so popular with residents and visitors today, was originally constructed in 1875 and called the "plank walk." It cut the distance to the beach from the heavily settled Jarvesville section of the village and allowed farmers to have access to the marsh pasturage along Town Neck. *The Acorn: Journal of the Sandwich Glass Museum* Volume 14, 2006/2007, page 15.

■ ■ ■

The thriving poultry business that flourished on the Cape in the late 19th century can be seen in this notice. In March of 1882, a train left from the Yarmouth station with 480 dozen eggs. *Yarmouth Register*, March 25, 1882.

■ ■ ■

This short item sounds very much like the beginning of a mathematics word problem: "An Orleans woman had from five hens in July 108 eggs. After killing one, the remaining four laid 90 eggs in August." Perhaps this should have concluded with something like: If she kills a second hen, how many eggs can she expect to receive in September? *Barnstable Patriot*, November 23, 1914.

■ ■ ■

At a meeting of the Brewster Lyceum in the winter of 1890, a question was opened for debate: "Resolved that in the majority of cases, the wife is the head of the family." The issue was argued in the affirmative by Mr. Joseph Newcomb. Mr. Herbert Foster took the negative view. Others who voiced opinions during the debate were Frank Crocker, John Clark, Charles Briggs, Isaac Clark, and Captain Freeman Snow. The question was decided with fifteen votes in the affirmative and thirteen votes in the negative. *Yarmouth Register*, February 8, 1890.

■ ■ ■

There was a lot of snow in the winter of 1896. After a Saturday of reckless speeding by sleigh drivers who took Jarves Street in Sandwich for a racetrack, the editor of the *Bourne Pioneer* newspaper was at least willing to make excuses for the offenders by noting that "racing is prohibited but parties are liable to forget the local laws when being pursued by a trotter whose driver is desirous of taking the lead; and instances of this kind were numerous on this occasion." *Bourne Pioneer*, January 14, 1896.

■ ■ ■

Archibald of Arabia: "The lecture, which was given at the (West Dennis) church on Wednesday evening, March 1, by Mr. Archibald Forder was fairly well attended, and gave an interesting glimpse into the ways of the Arabs, their peculiarities and their racial prejudices. Mr. Forder was in Arab costume, and related many interesting personal experiences which befell him during his thirteen years among the dwellers in tents." *Yarmouth Register*, March 11, 1905.

■ ■ ■

At one time, Cape Cod cows ate fish! Prior to the passage of a Massachusetts law that prohibited the owners of cows from grazing on the grass along shore, cows in Provincetown roamed freely among the beaches and dunes. They were attracted to the shore where fishermen were cleaning their catch. The animals at the Cape tip developed a taste for the entrails and in fact, to supplement their diets, their owners would mix minced fish in with their fodder to get them used to eating it. *"The Fish-Eating Cows of Provincetown, Massachusetts,"* by Isaac Hinckley, from a letter dated July 20, 1881 and published in the Bulletin of the United States Fish Commission, 1881, page 134.

■ ■ ■

During Prohibition, a meal served in a restaurant was called a "Cold Water Dinner" in the absence of an alcoholic beverage to go with it.

■ ■ ■

In 1931, selectmen in the town of Mashpee had the phone taken out of the town office because the lock on the door to the building was poor and too many citizens were going in at night and making personal calls. *Yarmouth Register*, March 26, 1932.

108

■ ■ ■

Eleanor Early, who wrote the book, *And This is Cape Cod*, published in 1936 by Houghton Mifflin Co., had quite an experience in the Caribbean while researching another travel piece. She was covering a night wild boar hunt in Trinidad and had climbed up into a tree to watch for the animal. She was seized there by a large python that wrapped itself around her. Unable to cry out, she had the presence of mind to turn on her flashlight. The light brought other hunters who dispatched the large snake with a machete. The Ever-Ready Battery Company heard about the story and featured the adventurous Ms. Early in one of its commercials, touting the reliability of its product. She told a reporter later that she had never encountered anything like it on Old Cape Cod. *"An Adventurous Life Examined,"* by Denise Taylor, *Boston Globe*, July 6, 2006

■ ■ ■

The 1938 Chatham annual town meeting warrant carried an article to appropriate $50.00 for the Shipwrecked Sailors Fund. Most towns on the outer Cape had always included such a yearly expenditure because of the number of wrecks that occurred on the Atlantic side. Chatham was the last town to continue the tradition. From Chatham town records.

■ ■ ■

An "anchor frost" happens when the top layer of surface water cools rapidly and then sinks, causing a bottom freeze that can kill shellfish. Though the surface water is not frozen, in such a case, the bottom water becomes frozen. From a Tales of Cape Cod interview with Olin J. Kelley of Waquoit, January 12, 1978.

■ ■ ■

At a special meeting of the Falmouth school committee in September of 1939, it was decreed that any future hiring of women teachers would include a contractual agreement that if they were to marry, they would have to resign. This rule would apply even if the woman had taught in the Falmouth schools for three years and had achieved tenure. The chairman of the school committee explained that, "We do not wish to overpopulate the teaching ranks with married women and thereby reduce opportunity and incentive." *Falmouth Enterprise*, September 8, 1939.

■ ■ ■

Helena Rubinstein, the famous beauty specialist, once owned property in Provincetown. In the fall of 1942, she purchased three houses at 40, 41, and 42 Commercial Street. The properties included a wharf and two cabins. *Yarmouth Register*, January 1, 1943.

■ ■ ■

Today, it would seem that everyone is happy about the creation of the Cape Cod National Seashore Park. Thousands of acres of land have been protected from development and the park has become a central tourist attraction. But when the park was in the planning stage, there were many on Cape Cod who thought it was a bad idea. Typical of that attitude is the following letter that was sent to the *Yarmouth Register* in April of 1959.

"Sir:

I am a native of Orleans and have lived here all my life and I would sure hate to see us overrun with campers and hot dog stands, which is what will happen if the park is fostered *[sic]* on us. I have been a member of the planning board here since it was voted several years ago and have always worked to preserve the Cape as a place that will be attractive to people to come as permanent residents. So you think the proposed park will do this? Do you know of anyone being refused the use of our ocean beach? The only place I know about is at Camp Wellfleet and Monomoy that the government owns now. Why don't you print a picture of the no trespass sign at the entrance to Monomoy beach? I think the park will be fatal to the economy of the lower Cape unless we want to run a pizza or hot dog stand. At present, we are building a Regional School with Wellfleet and Eastham that will cost 1-½ million dollars. How do you think we can pay for this with 75 percent of our taxes gone? I think some of you editorial writers better come down out of the clouds and see what is going on. Sure, let's have a national park, but let's have it in Yarmouth and Barnstable where the people want one.

Yours Truly,

Alton Smith, Orleans"

■ ■ ■

Always a strong Republican area, Cape Codders didn't think much of Social Security when it was introduced in the 1930's by the Franklin Roosevelt administration. "Somehow Cape Codders never took very kindly to the philosophy of spending more than they earned and mortgaging their future for alleged benefits of the present," wrote Lemuel C. Hall in the February 1938 edition of the *Cape Cod*

Beacon. "They have always considered a dollar in the bank to be an anchor to the windward and have relied more on good strong moorings for their financial crafts than on the moonbeams which so often precede a storm."

■ ■ ■

Under the headline "Properly Trained," comes this short news item: "The other day, Mrs. John F. Kennedy and daughter, Caroline, were enjoying a picnic lunch on a stretch of private beach in Hyannis Port. One little girl wandered away from her friends and stood aside, watching the progress of the diners. When Mrs. Kennedy offered her a few grapes or a piece of cake she shook her head and gravely replied: 'No, thank you. My mother won't let me take anything from strangers.'" *Barnstable Patriot,* July 19, 1962.

■ ■ ■

A Cape Cod sea captain was blessed with five daughters. As was the custom in the day, he named them Desire, Hopeful, Patience, Deliverance, and Thankful. As they grew into beautiful young women, there were many suitors calling at the house. One evening, a young man came to see one of the girls. One of the sisters, Patience, was sitting at the table knitting. "Young man," said the captain. "You are undoubtedly hopeful, and I suspect full of desire, but you will have to be thankful to wait with Patience until Deliverance comes." An old Cape Cod tale from *Cape Cod Almanac,* by Jack Johnson. Page 13.

■ ■ ■

From the April 14, 1877 *Provincetown Advocate* comes this poignant story of the aftermath of a spring storm. "We saw a father, who had two sons among the missing, for days and weeks, go morning and evening to the hill-top which overlooked the ocean, and there seating himself, would watch for hours, scanning the distant horizon with his glass, hoping every moment to discover some speck on which to build a hope."

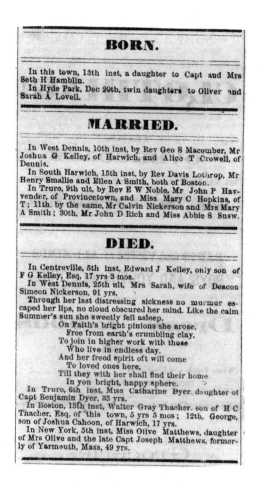

BORN.

In this town, 13th inst, a daughter to Capt and Mrs Seth H Hamblin.

In Hyde Park, Dec 20th, twin daughters to Oliver and Sarah A Lovell.

MARRIED.

In West Dennis, 10th inst, by Rev Geo S Macomber, Mr Joshua G Kelley, of Harwich, and Alice T Crowell, of Dennis.

In South Harwich, 15th inst, by Rev Davis Lothrop, Mr Henry Smallie and Ellen A Smith, both of Boston.

In Truro, 9th ult, by Rev E W Noble, Mr John P Havvender, of Provincetown, and Miss Mary C Hopkins, of T; 11th, by the same, Mr Calvin Nickerson and Mrs Mary A Smith; 30th, Mr John D Rich and Miss Abbie S Snsw.

DIED.

In Centreville, 5th inst, Edward J Kelley, only son of F G Kelley, Esq, 17 yrs 3 mos.

In West Dennis, 25th ult, Mrs Sarah, wife of Deacon Simeon Nickerson, 91 yrs.

Through her last distressing sickness no murmur escaped her lips, no cloud obscured her mind. Like the calm Summer's sun she sweetly fell asleep.

On Faith's bright pinions she arose,
Free from earth's crumbling clay,
To join in higher work with those
Who live in endless day.
And her freed spirit oft will come
To loved ones here,
Till they with her shall find their home
In yon bright, happy sphere.

In Truro, 6th inst, Miss Catharine Dyer, daughter of Capt Benjamin Dyer, 33 yrs.

In Boston, 13th inst, Walter Gray Thacher, son of H C Thacher, Esq, of this town, 5 yrs 5 mos; 12th, George, son of Joshua Cahoon, of Harwich, 17 yrs.

In New York, 5th inst, Miss Olive Matthews, daughter of Mrs Olive and the late Capt Joseph Matthews, formerly of Yarmouth, Mass, 49 yrs.

The essentials of a Cape Cod life – birth, marriage and death, as listed in the *Yarmouth Register* of February 18, 1870.

CHAPTER 16
Notable Quotables

If famous people had known that what they said would be written down and later quoted, they might have been more careful with their words. But then again, if they had been so thoughtful, perhaps they never would have become famous at all. Here are some quotes said by some famous and a few not so famous people on the subject of Cape Cod.

■ ■ ■

"But to omite other things (that I may be breefe) after longe beating at sea they fell with that land which is called Cape Cod; the which being made and certainly knowne to be it, they were not a litle joyful." *Of Plimoth Plantation*, by William Bradford.

■ ■ ■

Gabriel Archer, who was on board the ship *Concord* in the spring of 1602 with Captain Bartholomew Gosnold, described how Cape Cod got its name. "The fifteenth day we had again sight of land, which made ahead, being as we thought an island, by reason of a large sound that appeared westward between it and the main for coming to the west end whereof we did perceive a large opening, we called it Shoal Hope. Near this cape we came to anchor in fifteen fathoms, which we took great store of Cod-fish, for which we altered the name, and called it Cape Cod." From *The Relation of Captain Gosnold's Voyage to the North Part of Virginia.*

■ ■ ■

Prominent eighteenth century Congregational minister Timothy Dwight visited Cape Cod in the early 19th century. In his journal entitled, *Travels in New England and New York*, published in 1822, he observed the area of Orleans and Eastham. "The impression of this landscape cannot be realized without experience. It was a compound of wildness, gloom, and solitude. I felt myself transported to the borders of Nubia... A troop of Bedouins would have finished the picture..."

■ ■ ■

"The time must come when this coast will be a place of resort for those New-Englanders who really wish to visit the seaside...A man may stand there and put all America behind him." *Cape Cod*, by Henry David Thoreau

■ ■ ■

"When men are lost on the beach, the whole Cape takes it very much to heart, talks about it, mulls over it; when men are saved, there is no place where they are treated with more hospitality and kindness." *The Outermost House*, by Henry Beston.

■ ■ ■

"Cape Cod, on this showing, was exactly a pendant, pictured Japanese screen or banner; a delightful little triumph of 'impressionism,' which, during my short visit at least, never departed, under any provocation, from its type." American author Henry James on a visit to Cape Cod in 1906. *Sand in Their Shoes*, by Edith & Frank Shay, page 349.

■ ■ ■

"He was a native of Cape Cod; and hence, according to local usage, was called a Cape-Cod-man. A happy-go-lucky; neither craven nor valiant; taking perils as they came with an indifferent air; and while engaged in the most imminent crisis of the chase, toiling away, calm and collected as a journeyman joiner engaged for the year." *Moby Dick*, by Herman Melville.

■ ■ ■

That the Cape tip was an important art colony in the 1920's can be seen in the following from one of Hemingway's great works: "In California he fell among literary people and, as he still had a little of the fifty thousand left, in a short time he was backing a review of the Arts. The review commenced publication in Carmel, California, and finished in Provincetown, Massachusetts." *The Sun Also Rises*, by Ernest Hemingway.

■ ■ ■

"It has been said that Cape Codders by birth rather than adoption have salt in their hair, sand between their toes, and herring blood in their veins. Of these they never wholly rid themselves, nor do they want to..." *Now I Remember*, by children's author Thornton Burgess.

■ ■ ■

"This Cape is made by the main sea on the one side and a great bay on the other in forme of a sickle..." An account by Captain John Smith as he saw Cape Cod in 1614. *A Description of New England*, published in England in 1616.

■ ■ ■

"Where joyous porpoises roll and prank like clowns.
My shack standing in the middle
Of all this, in the midmost
Of the leagues of sand, of the long rolling leagues,
Next door to heaven and close on the gates of sunset,
The opening doors of dawn:
I've got what few have, I've got the life I want!"
"A Satisfactory Life," by Harry Kemp,
the Poet of the Provincetown Dunes.

■ ■ ■

"...Only a few people in the village were born on Cape Cod. Just as petrified wood is formed as minerals slowly replace organic material, so the present-day Barnstable has been formed by people from Evanston and Louisville and Boston and Pittsburgh and God-only-knows-where-else slowly replacing authentic rural Yankees." *"You've Never Been to Barnstable?"* by Kurt Vonnegut, Jr., printed in *Venture Magazine*, 1964.

■ ■ ■

"The Cape man may get beyond, but he never gets over, the Cape. It colors him all his life, the root and fiber of him" *A Trip Around Cape Cod*, by E.G. Perry, 1898.

■ ■ ■

"Doctor [Richard] Bourne was temperate in his habits; that is he never was intoxicated at his own expense." An account of the Bourne family as written by Amos Otis in *Genealogical Notes of Barnstable Families*, 1979 edition, page 122.

■ ■ ■

"Jack N. was to have sent someone today to mow the grass; instead, he phoned to say he'd send someone tomorrow. I know these Cape Cod tomorrows. Tomorrow is someday; it means not today. I did half the grass myself, which is the best way to be safe against a Cape Cod tomorrow." *Journal for Josephine*, by Robert Nathan, page 123.

■ ■ ■

"Some of the characteristics of the beach grass seem also to be characteristics of the people of the Cape. They have the same hardiness and endurance, and like the beach grass, have adapted themselves to their environment and thrive where most would fail." "Cape Cod Folks," by Clifton Johnson, published in *New England Magazine*, August, 1902.

■ ■ ■

"Yes, our Cape Cod is still a place for the good citizen and it must continue to be just that." Cape Cod author Joseph Crosby Lincoln in the introduction to *About Cape Cod*, 1936.

■ ■ ■

Famous American painter and world traveler John Singer Sargent (1856-1925), after visiting Breakwater Beach in Brewster, said, "Of all places in the whole world, this is the most beautiful beach." *Brewster Reminiscences*, by Mary Olmstead Loud, recorded November 14, 1989, Brewster Ladies Library collection.

■ ■ ■

"They're not anxious that I should live in Sandwich, but I'll stay there yet." Words uttered by famous 19th century actor Joe Jefferson after local residents refused to sell him a house in town because he was an actor. He purchased a burial plot in town and in 1905, when he died, he was buried in Bayview cemetery on Route 130 – staying there yet!

Joe Jefferson in his prime.
Cape Cod Magazine, November 1915.

CHAPTER 17
Last Words

*For many, the graveyard epitaph is the final word. Our Cape Cod ceme-
teries are filled with inscriptions that run the gamut from the very poignant
and hopeful to the intentionally—or perhaps unintentionally humorous.
Actor W.C. Fields made it clear that other things being equal, in the end
he would have preferred to be in Philadelphia. Whether the people cited
below had time to reflect about being eternally planted on Cape Cod is not
known. But there is no doubt that the carved tributes on their headstones
say much of who they were and how they viewed life in their own time.*

■ ■ ■

JIM COOGAN PHOTO

The old Sandwich burying ground.

The year 1849 was a tragic one for Lewis and Appia Atwood of Wellfleet. On August 4th they lost their five-year-old son, Samuel. They buried him in the Duck Creek cemetery under the inscription:

"Said Jesus, now suffer little children to come
I'll bless and protect them and take them safe home.
Then grief stricken parents soar up with faith's eye
Your sweet little cherub, Sam'l now dwells in the sky."

Just five days later their son, Lewis, died at six years and eight months. The parents laid him next to his brother and had another poem inscribed on his stone:

"Since Sam has fled to the region of light
You, sweet Lewis, must go from our sight.
In life so brief, in death they can't part
Although so afflictive to a fond parent's heart."

On August 15, 1849, Lewis and Appia said a final good-bye to their ten-month-old daughter, Rachel. Completing the trilogy, the smallest stone said:

"Now Sam'l and Lewis have gone up on high
One more little cherub, sweet babe too must die
In one day their bodies were here laid away
To rest with their spirits at the great coming day."

Wellfleet, Truro & Cape Cod Cemetery Inscriptions Section #3: Duck Creek Cemetery, Wellfleet, Massachusetts, by Elizabeth Freeman, page DC 33.

■ ■ ■

Another stone that is a poignant reminder of how close death was in earlier times can be found in the West Barnstable burying ground off Route 149. When five-week-old Caroline Huckins died in 1795, her grieving parents wrote:

"Sleep on my babe and take thy rest.
God called thee home. He thought it best."

■ ■ ■

From the grave of Mary C. Dolencie, located in the Ancient Cemetery, Yarmouth Port, comes an angry curse:

"May eternal damnation be
upon those in Whaling Port
who without knowing me
have maliciously vilified me.
May the curse of God
Be upon them and theirs"

■ ■ ■

A Sudden Death: From the grave of Reuben Eldridge, East Harwich Cemetery:

"Stop my friends as you pass by
And view the place in which I lie:
And learn how sudden life has fled
At night in health, next morning dead"

■ ■ ■

Final verdict: Former attorney William Sinclaire West (1899 – 1962) left this message on his gravestone in the Mashpee Wampanoag Church burial ground:

"The Defense Rests"

■ ■ ■

The Howes cemetery off Beach Street in Dennis has a stone that speaks to the confidence of Obed Howes:

"Reason was his guiding star.
Whatever is, is right."

■ ■ ■

Azuba Handy, the first wife of Captain Bethuel G. Handy, was the first person buried in Mosswood Cemetery in Cotuit. She died in March of 1819. Her epitaph is a touching reminder of a loving wife and mother:

"My bosom friend come here and see
Where lays the last remains of me.
When I the debt of nature paid
A burying yard for me was made.
Here lays the body of your bride

The loving knot is now untied.
A loving husband you have been.
To me the dearest of all men.
Husband and children here I lay.
Stamp on your minds my dying day.
Come often here and take a view.
Where lays the one that loved you."

Cotuit – Some Notes on Her History, Barnstable Tercentenary Committee for Cotuit, 1939.

■ ■ ■

The Reverend Samuel Palmer had a long and productive ministry as pastor of the Falmouth Congregational Church. He died on April 15th, 1775, just four days before the battle of Lexington and Concord. His 45-year tenure as the town spiritual leader is summed up in two lines:

"His virtues would a monument supply.
But underneath these clods, his ashes lie."

Acknowledgements

A book of this type doesn't get completed without the help of a lot of people. I want to thank the many fine Cape Cod libraries and historical societies that have done such a wonderful job of preserving the history of our towns and villages. The willingness of these institutions to share information from their collections and their help in the search for materials is very much appreciated.

For the friends and associates that I've had the pleasure and privilege of working with in putting this book together, I offer a sincere thank you. In particular, the long connection that I've had with my co-writer, Jack Sheedy, is especially valued. I was always an historian. Jack is the person who made me a writer.

And as always, I'm indebted to the support and encouragement of my wife, Beth, who makes sure that I don't ever split an infinitive or forget to dot my i's and cross my t's.

First, I wish to recognize the many libraries, historical societies, and museums across the Cape that provided assistance to me over the years. These institutions of knowledge and learning are invaluable resources in the communities they serve and thankfully they are available for our use. May this always be the case.

A heartfelt thank you to friends and family who have showed an interest in my work. My wife, Adriana, and children, Melissa and Gregory, have always been most supportive, and continue to provide useful commentary and advice. Once again, my sincere gratitude goes to Jim Coogan, my co-author, publisher, and friend, with whom I have shared many a cup of coffee over the years as we plan our literary adventures.

Finally, I wish to thank those from centuries and generations ago who created the history that continues to warrant our remembrance. Hopefully, those of us who now populate this current generation will learn a thing or two from those who came before.

We want to especially thank Kristen vonHentschel for her work in designing *Cape Odd*. We were fortunate to have her professional expertise in completing the book.

About the Authors

Jim Coogan is a well-known Cape Cod historian. An award-winning author (*Sail Away Ladies: Stories of Cape Cod Women in the Age of Sail*)*, he is a frequent lecturer and commentator on topics related to the Cape. Raised in the town of Brewster in the birthplace home of Cape Cod novelist Joseph Crosby Lincoln, Jim was grounded at an early age in the wonderful history and lore of this famous peninsula. He has written seven books filled with stories and tales about Cape Cod for children and adults. Retired after almost three decades as a high school history teacher, Jim is a regular columnist for the *Cape Cod Times* daily newspaper. This is his fourth collaboration with Dennis author Jack Sheedy. He lives in Sandwich with his wife Beth.

Jack Sheedy is the author of six books and of more than 500 published articles. His books include *Cape Cod Harvest*, written with Jim Coogan, and *Dennis Journal*, which he co-published with the Dennis Historical Society. He has written freelance for 25 years. Over that time, he has served on the writing team of the *Barnstable Patriot*'s annual history magazine, *Summerscape* – issues of which have thrice been awarded first place for editorial excellence by the New England Press Association.** Jack has written copy for a number of Massachusetts businesses and organizations, including the John F. Kennedy Library in Boston. He has appeared on HGTV and NPR radio, speaking about Cape Cod history and lore. Jack and his family live in Dennis.

* United States Maritime Literature Award – 2004
** New England Press Association (NEPA) – 1995, 1999, 2008

Bibliography

Anonymous. *Mourt's Relation*. Boston, MA: J.K. Wiggin, 1865. (Note: Generally attributed to Pilgrims William Bradford and Edward Winslow)

Barnstable County. *Three Centuries of a Cape Cod County: Barnstable, Massachusetts, 1685-1985*. Barnstable, MA: Barnstable County, 1985.

Barnstable Tercentenary Committee for Cotuit. *Cotuit–Some Notes on Her History*. Hyannis, MA: F.B. & F.P. Goss, 1939.

Beston, Henry, *The Outermost House*. New York, NY: Holt, Rinehart & Winston, 1960.

Bradford, William. *Bradford's History "Of Plimoth Plantation."* Boston, MA: Wright & Potter Printing Co, 1898.

Buckley, Joseph. *Wings Over Cape Cod*. Orleans, MA: Lower Cape Pub., 2000.

Burgess, Thornton. *Now I Remember*. Boston, MA: Little Brown, 1960.

Clinton, Bill. *My Life*. New York, NY: Alfred A. Knopf, 2004.

Cole, Stephen and Lindy Gifford. *The Cranberry: Hard Work and Holiday Sauce*. Gardiner, ME: Tilbury House, 2009.

Cullity, Rosanna and John Nye. *A Sandwich Album*. East Sandwich, MA: Nye Family of America Association, 1987.

Dalton, J.W. *The Lifesavers of Cape Cod*. Chatham, MA: The Chatham Press, Inc., 1967.

Deyo, Simeon L. *History of Barnstable County, Massachusetts 1620-1890*. New York, NY: H.W. Blake & Co, 1890.

Digges, Jeremiah (Josef Berger). *Cape Cod Pilot*. Provincetown, MA & New York, NY: Modern Pilgrim Press and Viking Press, 1937.

Dwight, Timothy. *Travels in New England and New York*. New Haven, CT: Timothy Dwight., S. Converse Printer, 1822.

Early, Eleanor. *And This is Cape Cod*. Boston, MA: Houghton Mifflin Company, 1936.

Farson, Robert. *Cape Cod Railroads*. Yarmouth Port, MA: Cape Cod Historical Publications, 1990.

Farson, Robert. *The Cape Cod Canal*. Middletown, CT: Wesleyan University Press, 1977.

Freeman, Frederick. *The History of Cape Cod*. Yarmouth Port, MA: Parnassus Imprints, 1965.

Gelb, Arthur and Barbara. *O'Neill*. New York, NY: Harper, 1962.

Geller, L.D. *Sea Serpents of Coastal New England*. Plymouth, MA: Cape Cod Publications, 1979.

Harwich Historical Commission. *Harwich Men of the Sea*. Harwich, MA: Harwich Historical Commission, 1977.

Heavey, William. *Down Ramp: The Story of the Army Amphibian Engineers*. Washington, DC: Infantry Journal Press, 1947.

Hemingway, Ernest. *The Sun Also Rises*. New York, NY: Scribner, 1995.

Hinshaw, John. *Marconi and His South Wellfleet Wireless*. Chatham, MA: Chatham Press, 1969.

Holly, H.H. *Sparrow-hawk: A Seventeenth Century Vessel in Twentieth Century America*. Boston, MA: The Nimrod Press, 1969.

Hutchins, Francis G. *Mashpee: The Story of Cape Cod's Indian Town*. West Franklin, NH: Amarta Press, 1979.

Johnson, Jack. *Cape Cod Almanac*. Yarmouth Port, MA: Jack Johnson, 1945.

Kittredge, George Lyman. *Witchcraft in Old and New England*. Cambridge, MA: Harvard University Press, 1929.

Kittredge, Henry C. *Cape Cod: Its People & Their History*. Boston, MA: Houghton Mifflin Company, 1968.

Kittredge, Henry C. *Mooncussers of Cape Cod*. Hamden, CT: Archon Books, 1971.

Lincoln, Joseph C. *Cape Cod Yesterdays*. New York, NY: Blue Ribbon Books, 1939.

Lovell, Jr., R.A. *Sandwich – A Cape Cod Town*. Sandwich, MA: Town of Sandwich Archives & Historical Center, 1984.

Marshall, Anthony L. *Truro, Cape Cod, As I Knew It*. New York, NY: Vantage Press, 1974.

McLean, Sally Pratt. *Cape Cod Folks*. Boston, MA: DeWolfe, Fiske & Co., 1881.

Melville, Herman. *Moby Dick*. New York, NY: Knopf: Random House, 1991.

Moffett, Ross. *Art in Narrow Streets*. Falmouth, MA: Kendall Print Co., 1964.

Nathan, Robert. *Journal for Josephine*. New York, NY: A.A. Knopf, 1943.

Otis, Amos. *Genealogical Notes of Barnstable Families*. Barnstable, MA: F.B. & F.P. Goss Publishers and Printers, 1888.

Perry, E.G. *A Trip Around Cape Cod*. Boston, MA: C.S. Binner, 1898.

Pratt, Ambrose E. *Two Hundred and Fiftieth Anniversary Celebration of Sandwich and Bourne at Sandwich, Massachusetts*. Falmouth, MA: Local Pub & Print Co., 1890.

Quinn, William. *Cape Cod Maritime Disasters*. Orleans, MA: Lower Cape Publishing, 1990.

Quinn, William. *Shipwrecks Around Cape Cod*. Orleans, MA: Lower Cape Publishing, 1973.

Reid, Nancy Thacher. *Dennis,*

Cape Cod. Dennis, MA: Dennis Historical Society, 1996.

Reynard, Elizabeth. *The Narrow Land.* Chatham, MA: Chatham Historical Society, 1978.

Renehan, Jr., Edward. *The Kennedys at War: 1937 – 1945.* New York, NY: Doubleday, 2002.

Rich, Frederick S. (editor), Elizabeth Freeman & others. *Wellfleet, Truro & Cape Cod Cemetery Inscriptions Section #3: Duck Creek Cemetery, Wellfleet, Massachusetts.* Wellfleet, MA: Rich Family Association, 1983.

Salinger, Pierre. *With Kennedy.* Garden City, NY: Doubleday, 1966.

Shay, Edith & Frank. *Sand in Their Shoes.* Boston, MA: Houghton Mifflin, 1951.

Skeyhill, Thomas. *Soldier Songs from Anzac.* Melbourne: George Robertson & Co., 1916.

Sloane, Eric. *A Reverence for Wood.* New York, NY: Ballantine Books, 1973.

Small, Isaac M. *Shipwrecks on Cape Cod.* Chatham, MA: The Chatham Press, Inc., 1967.

Snow, Edward Rowe. *A Pilgrim Returns to Cape Cod.* Boston, MA: The Yankee Publishing Co., 1946.

State Street Company. *Some Merchants and Sea Captains of Old Boston.* Boston, MA: State Street Trust Company, 1919.

Strandwold, Olaf. *Norse Inscriptions on American Stones.* Weehauken, NJ: M. Bjorndal, 1948.

Swift, Charles F. *Cape Cod: The Right Arm of Massachusetts: An Historical Narrative.* Yarmouth, MA: Register Pub. Co., 1987.

Swift, Charles F. *History of Old Yarmouth.* Yarmouthport, MA: The Historical Society of Old Yarmouth, 1975.

Theriault, James. *Every First Monday: A History of King Hiram's Lodge, Provincetown and Its Members.* Provincetown. MA, 1995.

Thoreau, Henry David. *Cape Cod.* New York, NY: Bramhall House, 1951.

Trayser, Donald G. *Barnstable: Three Centuries of a Cape Cod Town.* Hyannis, MA: F.B. & F.P. Goss, 1939.

Various. *About Cape Cod.* Boston, MA: Thomas Todd Co., 1936.

Vorse, Mary Heaton. *Time and the Town: A Provincetown Chronicle.* New York, NY: Dial Press, 1942.

Vuilleumier, Marion. *Churches on Cape Cod.* Taunton, MA: W. S. Sullwold Publishing, 1974.

Williams, Lenore Wheeler. *Sandwich Glass.* Bridgeport, CT: The Park City Eng. Co., 1922.

Willison, George P. *Saints & Strangers.* New York, NY: Time, Inc., 1964.

Wilson, Charles Morrow. *Dow Baker and the Great Banana Fleet.* Harrisburg, PA: Stackpole Books, 1972.

Wood, William. *New England's Prospect.* Amherst, MA: University of Massachusetts Press, 1977.

Woods Hole, Martha's Vineyard and Nantucket Steamship Authority. *Lifeline to the Islands: Sketches* and *Memories of Steamers Past and Present on the Woods Hole – Martha's Vineyard – Nantucket Run.* Woods Hole, MA: Woods Hole, Martha's Vineyard and Nantucket Steamship Authority, 1977.

Other Published Sources:

Records of the Plymouth Colony: Judicial Acts 1636-1692, 1877 Edition, printed by the press of William White, Boston, MA.

Plymouth Colony: Court Orders: 1678-1694, 1856 Edition, printed by the press of William White, Boston, MA.

"The Case of Bathsheba Spooner," in *American Antiquarian Society Proceedings*, Volume 5, October 1888.

"History of the Original Congregational Church in Sandwich," from a series of articles published in the *Yarmouth Register*, May 5 & August 11, 1877.

"A History of the Congregational Church of South Dennis," compiled by G. Kenneth Rogers, church historian, 1992.

Sketch of the Third Baptist Church and Meeting House with Membership Enrollment, by Lizzie S. (Hinckley) Crocker, published in 1927.

The Acorn: Journal of the Sandwich Glass Museum, Volume 14, 2006/2007.

"The Fish-Eating Cows of Provincetown, Massachusetts," by Isaac Hinckley, from a letter dated July 20, 1881 and published in the *Bulletin of the United States Fish Commission*, 1881.

The Relations of Captain Gosnold's Voyage to the North Part of Virginia, by Gabriel Archer, 1602.

A Description of New England, by Captain John Smith, published in England in 1616. Also published in Boston, MA by W. Veazie, 1865.

The Mayflower Quarterly, September 2000.

Newspapers & Magazines:
Barnstable Enterprise
Barnstable Patriot
Boston Globe
Boston Transcript
Bourne Pioneer
Cape Cod Beacon
Cape Cod Bee
Cape Cod Magazine
Cape Cod News
Cape Cod Standard Times
Cape Cod Voice
Evening Ledger, Philadelphia
Falmouth Enterprise
Harper's Magazine
Harwich Independent
Hyannis Patriot
New England Magazine
New York Times
Niles Weekly Register
Register
Sandwich Independent
Sandwich Observer
Yarmouth Register